VMware Workstation – No Experience Necessary

Get started with VMware Workstation to create virtual machines and a virtual testing platform

Sander van Vugt

BIRMINGHAM - MUMBAI

VMware Workstation – No Experience Necessary

First published: August 2013

Production Reference: 1160813

Published by Packt Publishing Ltd.
Livery Place
35 Livery Street
Birmingham B3 2PB, UK.

ISBN 978-1-84968-918-2

www.packtpub.com

Cover Image by Duraid Fatouhi (duraidfatouhi@yahoo.com)

Credits

Author
Sander van Vugt

Reviewers
Sean Duffy
Frederik Vos

Acquisition Editors
Andrew Duckworth
Julian Ursell

Commissioning Editor
Sharvari Tawde

Technical Editors
Vrinda Nitesh Bhosale
Pratik More

Copy Editors
Gladson Monteiro
Insiya Morbiwala
Alfida Paiva
Laxmi Subramanian

Project Coordinator
Amey Sawant

Proofreader
Jenny Blake

Indexer
Tejal Soni

Graphics
Ronak Dhruv

Production Coordinator
Arvindkumar Gupta

Cover Work
Arvindkumar Gupta

About the Author

Sander van Vugt is an independent author, consultant, and technical trainer, living in Netherlands. He is specialized in open source software and virtualization. He has written over 50 books on many subjects, most of them about Linux. As a consultant he has realized numerous projects involving open source software and virtualization for different companies around the world. You can find more information about him on his website, www.sandervanvugt.com.

About the Reviewers

Sean Duffy is a virtualization evangelist, programmer, and general technical enthusiast living in the South West of England. He has worked in the virtualization and cloud computing space since circa 2007, garnering an appreciation and enjoyment of the technologies surrounding these industries.

Thriving off of helping others, Sean enjoys sharing knowledge around the technical topics he is most enthused about. Over the last five years he has run a blog, Shogan.tech, discussing ideas, projects, and technical articles covering topics such as Virtualization, Scripting, and Automation. He is also an author on the popular technical journal and community hub website, Simple-Talk, and runs a second blog dedicated to his passion for creating games and programming.

He holds various Virtualization and Cloud certifications, and has been awarded the title VMware vExpert for the years 2012 and 2013.

Sean is currently working as a Technical Consultant for Xtravirt Limited in the United Kingdom, where he enjoys exposure to many different technologies across the Virtualization, Cloud and End User Computing stacks.

> I would like to thank my wife, Carmen for her support and patience over the years I have spent chasing my passion for technology.

Frederik Vos, living in Berkenwoude, a small town near Gouda in Netherlands, has been working as a senior technical trainer of virtualization technologies, such as Citrix XenServer, and VMware vSphere. He has specialized in data center infrastructures (hypervisor, network, and storage) and cloud computing (cloudstack, cloudplatform, and openstack). He is also a Linux trainer and evangelist. He has a lot of knowledge as a teacher and also real-world experience as a system engineer.

For the last six years Frederik is working for XTG in Gouda, a training-center specialized in virtualization and Linux. XTG is one of the biggest VMWare authorized training center (VATC) in Netherlands, and has received several awards from both VMware and Citrix.

www.PacktPub.com

Support files, eBooks, discount offers and more

You might want to visit www.PacktPub.com for support files and downloads related to your book.

Did you know that Packt offers eBook versions of every book published, with PDF and ePub files available? You can upgrade to the eBook version at www.PacktPub.com and as a print book customer, you are entitled to a discount on the eBook copy. Get in touch with us at service@packtpub.com for more details.

At www.PacktPub.com, you can also read a collection of free technical articles, sign up for a range of free newsletters and receive exclusive discounts and offers on Packt books and eBooks.

http://PacktLib.PacktPub.com

Do you need instant solutions to your IT questions? PacktLib is Packt's online digital book library. Here, you can access, read and search across Packt's entire library of books.

Why Subscribe?
- Fully searchable across every book published by Packt
- Copy and paste, print and bookmark content
- On demand and accessible via web browser

Free Access for Packt account holders

If you have an account with Packt at www.PacktPub.com, you can use this to access PacktLib today and view nine entirely free books. Simply use your login credentials for immediate access.

Instant Updates on New Packt Books

Get notified! Find out when new books are published by following @PacktEnterprise on Twitter, or the *Packt Enterprise* Facebook page.

Table of Contents

Preface

VMware is the world leader in virtualization solutions. VMware offers products to virtualize the data center, and also solutions that help you set up test environments. This book is about VMware Workstation, the most versatile solution that can be used to set up a test environment to develop new software solutions, or to test complex architecture before taking it into production.

What this book covers

Chapter 1, Installing VMware Workstation, explains how to install VMware Workstation on Windows or Linux computers. It also describes the recommended hardware to set up a virtualization environment.

Chapter 2, Installing Virtual Machines, describes what to do before even starting the installation of the first virtual machine, such as setting up storage or networking. It also explains how to create different types of virtual machines.

Chapter 3, Working with Virtual Machines, shows you how to get around and perform some of the most common tasks in VMware Workstation as VMware Workstation offers several options to make it easier to work with virtual machines.

Chapter 4, VMware Workstation behind the Scenes, describes how VMware Workstation is organized. It teaches you about the different files that are used, and the processes in use to offer all of the required services.

Chapter 5, Networking VMware Workstation, shows how to set up the different types of network that can be used in VMware Workstation environments.

Chapter 6, Accessing Virtual Machines Remotely, teaches you how to access virtual machines from a distance, using solutions such as the integrated web server that you can use.

Chapter 7, Converting Virtual Machines, shows how to convert virtual machines, which help you to import virtual machines that have been created on other virtualization platforms.

Chapter 8, Cloning and Snapshots, teaches you how to work with clones and snapshots, which allow you to set up a test environment in an easy and versatile way.

Chapter 9, Sharing Virtual Machines, teaches you how to share virtual machines. It also covers how to easily share the machines that you've created with other people you want to work with.

What you need for this book

To learn how to work with VMware Workstation, you need a copy of VMware Workstation. This can be obtained from www.vmware.com.

Who this book is for

This book is written for system administrators and developers who want to set up test environments to verify the working of new products in isolated and secure environments.

Conventions

In this book, you will find a number of styles of text that distinguish between different kinds of information. Here are some examples of these styles, and an explanation of their meaning.

Code words in text, database table names, folder names, filenames, file extensions, pathnames, dummy URLs, user input, and Twitter handles are shown as follows: "The entire configuration of the virtual machine is specified in the .vmx file".

A block of code is set as follows:

```
# Disk DescriptorFile
version=1
encoding="UTF-8"
CID=bb3b482f
parentCID=ffffffff
```

Any command-line input or output is written as follows:

```
inet6 fe80::250:56ff:fec0:8/64 scope link
    valid_lft forever preferred_lft forever
```

New terms and **important words** are shown in bold. Words that you see on the screen, in menus or dialog boxes, for example, appear in the text like this: "Click on **Add Network** to add a new network".

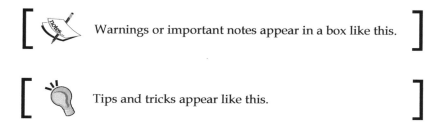

[Warnings or important notes appear in a box like this.]

[Tips and tricks appear like this.]

Reader feedback

Feedback from our readers is always welcome. Let us know what you think about this book—what you liked or may have disliked. Reader feedback is important for us to develop titles that you really get the most out of.

To send us general feedback, simply send an e-mail to feedback@packtpub.com, and mention the book title through the subject of your message.

If there is a topic that you have expertise in and you are interested in either writing or contributing to a book, see our author guide on www.packtpub.com/authors.

Customer support

Now that you are the proud owner of a Packt book, we have a number of things to help you to get the most from your purchase.

Errata

Although we have taken every care to ensure the accuracy of our content, mistakes do happen. If you find a mistake in one of our books—maybe a mistake in the text or the code—we would be grateful if you would report this to us. By doing so, you can save other readers from frustration and help us improve subsequent versions of this book. If you find any errata, please report them by visiting http://www.packtpub.com/support, selecting your book, clicking on the **errata submission form** link, and entering the details of your errata. Once your errata are verified, your submission will be accepted and the errata will be uploaded to our website, or added to any list of existing errata, under the Errata section of that title.

Piracy

Piracy of copyright material on the Internet is an ongoing problem across all media. At Packt, we take the protection of our copyright and licenses very seriously. If you come across any illegal copies of our works, in any form, on the Internet, please provide us with the location address or website name immediately so that we can pursue a remedy.

Please contact us at copyright@packtpub.com with a link to the suspected pirated material.

We appreciate your help in protecting our authors, and our ability to bring you valuable content.

Questions

You can contact us at questions@packtpub.com if you are having a problem with any aspect of the book, and we will do our best to address it.

1
Installing VMware Workstation

In this chapter, you'll learn how to install VMware Workstation. The chapter is not just about executing a wizard by clicking on next, next, and finish, you'll also learn how to configure the computer that will run VMware Workstation wisely and perform an advanced installation on either Windows or Linux.

Configuring the host computer

Before starting the installation of VMware Workstation, you should take care of the host computer on which you want to use VMware Workstation. Sure, any computer that meets the minimal requirements will work, but if you choose the appropriate configuration, you'll benefit more from your VMware Workstation installation. In this section, we'll spend a few words on using the most appropriate configuration for your computer.

CPU and CPU cores

Every virtual machine that you'll install will work as a computer by itself, and the total number of CPU cores in your computer will be available as the maximum number of CPUs that you'll allocate to a virtual machine. However, if you want to get the best performance out of your virtual machines, it is a good idea to not configure more virtual CPUs than the total number of CPUs and CPU cores in your computer. This means that if you have four cores in total, ideally you shouldn't run more than three virtual machines with one core each at the same time. As the number of virtual CPUs that are in use gets higher than the total number of CPUs in your computer, CPUs must be shared, and that is not good for performance.

There is no formal number of CPU cores, so if you're on a budget for hardware, you can run VMware Workstation on a computer that has only one core. However for best possible performance, this is not recommended.

Linux cgroups

If you are running VMware Workstation on Linux, you can use cgroups. With cgroups, you can define groups of resources that make sure that every VM always has a dedicated amount of system resources available; a nice and efficient way to use the hardware in the best and most optimal way.

Memory

If a computer runs out of physical RAM, it starts swapping to disk. Using VMware Workstation, you want to avoid your computer starting to swap at all times. To make sure this never happens, the total size of RAM in your computer must be more than the total amount of RAM in use by all the virtual machines, with an addition of 2 GB for the host operating system for smooth operation. This means that a typical computer that is going to be used for VMware Workstation will have at least 4 GB of RAM or more if possible. But if you're on a budget and want to create virtual machines that don't need much RAM, you can work with VMware Workstation on a minimal 1 GB of RAM.

Disk space

A very important part of the configuration of the host system is the available disk space. Typically, each virtual machine needs a couple of gigabytes of available disk space; so a minimal configuration will need at least 10 GB of available disk space, whereas on a dedicated test machine that is going to run several virtual machines, you might need hundreds of gigabytes of free disk space.

If you're looking for good performance, just having the available disk space is not enough. This is because you don't want the virtual machine disk file to be fragmented. To avoid fragmentation, it is recommended that you use a machine where a separate disk is dedicated to the storage of VMDK files. The benefit of this that you can avoid fragmentation, and you'll have one disk that is dedicated to the operating system and another disk that is dedicated to handling virtual machine I/O requests.

Getting VMware Workstation

To get VMware Workstation, you'll typically download it from www.vmware.com. From the VMware site, you can either download a trial version or purchase VMware Workstation. Once you've got the VMware installation file and a registration code, you can start the installation. You can also create an account at the VMware site that allows you to easily access all of your previous purchases. In this section, you'll learn how to buy your own copy of VMware Workstation and how to access purchased products from your VMware account.

Purchasing VMware Workstation

The following procedure describes how to get VMware Workstation:

Support

There is a supported version of VMware Workstation, but it is only available if you buy 10 licenses or more. If you're going to use VMware Workstation in a business environment and you want easy access to help, buy the supported version. VMware offers basic support that is 12 hours a day from Monday to Friday or business support that is 24 hours a day, 7 days a week. When purchasing support, you can select a contract period of either one year or three years. If support is important for you, I recommend that you buy Production support. The price difference is small, and for this small difference you will have 24/7 support.

1. Start a browser and go to www.vmware.com. Click on the **VMware Store** button and navigate to **Desktop Products | VMware Workstation 9**.

2. Select **Buy Now** if you have never bought VMware Workstation before. If you have a recent version, click on **Upgrade** to pay the discount price.

3. Enter the quantity of VMware Workstation licenses that you want to buy and click on **Add to Cart**. Your shopping cart will now be updated.

4. After indicating what you want to buy, click on **Secure Checkout** to pay for your VMware license. This brings you to a window where you can either log in with an existing VMware account or create a new VMware account and enter your billing information.

5. Click on **Continue** to complete the transaction. You'll now have access to your own version of VMware Workstation.

Setting up your VMware account

After your purchase of VMware Workstation, you can access your account to download it later from the VMware website. You can always download the software from here as well as access the associated license keys.

To access your account on www.vmware.com, click on **My Account** and log in with the e-mail address and password that you created when purchasing VMware Workstation. You'll also see a drop-down list (see the following screenshot) from which you can indicate what kind of information you're looking for. For instance, select **Login to Find Serial Numbers** to get your serial number from the VMware site. After logging in, you'll find a list of all the products that you've purchased as well as a link to download your version of VMware Workstation.

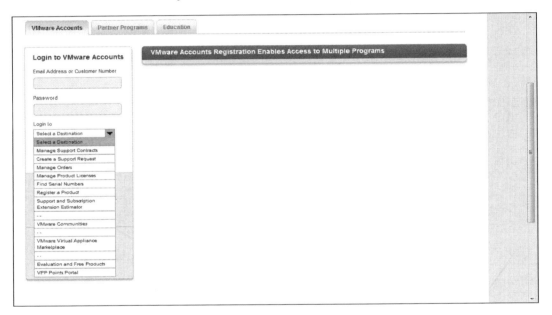

Downloading VMware Workstation

Once you've purchased VMware Workstation, the easiest way to download it is to go to the VMware website and select the **Product & Downloads** link. From here, you can select **VMware Workstation** and easily download the software.

Installing VMware Workstation on Windows

In this section, I'll assume that you've made all appropriate preparations to start the installation of VMware Workstation. This means that you have installed the Windows host operating system and purchased VMware Workstation and are all ready to start the installation. Perform the following steps:

1. Log in to the VMware website and select **Products & Downloads**. From there, select **Download VMware Workstation for Windows** and click on the **Manually Download** link. Accept the license agreement, which will start the download.

2. After downloading the installation file, double-click on it to run it. Allow the installation program to be executed when the Windows Security policy asks if you want to allow it. You will now see the first screen of the **VMware Workstation Setup** wizard. Click on **Next** to start the installation.

3. The installer now gives you the option to select between a typical installation and a custom installation. The typical installation doesn't need much explanation; therefore, in this book I'll explain the options that are presented by the custom installation procedure.

4. You'll now see a list of different program components that you can install. You should at least install the core components as they contain everything that is required to start VMware Workstation. If you want to develop your own tools to manage and monitor VMware Workstation's virtual machines, select the **VIX Application Programming Interface** (this typically only makes sense if you're a developer). The **Enhanced Keyboard Utility** is useful if you need easy access to virtual machines from computers that have a different keyboard layout.

Use the **Visual Studio Plugin** for the easy debugging of error messages generated by VMware Workstation.

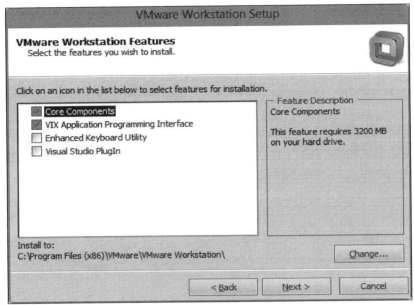

Select the options that you want to install

5. With VMware Workstation, you can provide access to your virtual machines using the Workstation Server. This server provides access to shared virtual machines by default over the secure HTTP port 443. In the following screenshot, you'll indicate where virtual machines are stored and on which port the Workstation Server Component will listen. If you want to change these two settings, you can do it here.

6. In the following window, the setup program asks if you want to check for product updates on startup. If you're using this option, you'll get notifications if a newer version is available. Following that there is an option where you will indicate if you want to send anonymous system data and usage statistics to VMware. This option is *On* by default, but you can deselect it here if you don't want to share your usage information with VMware. Following this window, you can indicate if you want shortcuts to launch VMware Workstation on the desktop and start menu's **All Programs** option.

7. After specifying what you want to do with these basic options, you can click on **Continue** to start the installation process. As about 3 gigabytes of files will be copied to your computer now, this will take some time to complete.

8. Once all files have been copied to your computer, you are prompted to enter a license key. You don't have to do that at this point; but you will need to enter the license key anyway before you can create your first virtual machine, so you might as well do it now.

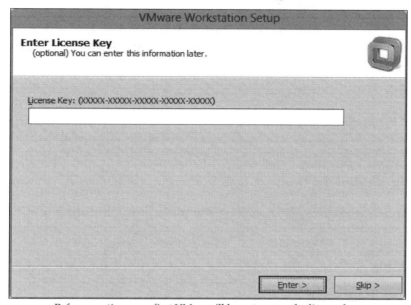

Before creating your first VM, you'll have to enter the license key

9. The installation is now complete. Click on **Finish** to close the setup wizard.

Installing VMware Workstation on Linux

Installing VMware Workstation on a Windows workstation isn't hard to do; just run the installation file and change a few of the default parameters and it will work. The installation of VMware on Linux is a bit more difficult because you'll have to run a few commands from a shell environment.

64 or 32 bits?

If you're using VMware on Linux, you should install a 64-bit flavour of Linux. The handling of hardware resources, especially memory, is much more efficient on a 64-bit Linux version than it is on a 32-bit version of Linux. So for the best possible performance, make sure to use the 64-bit Linux version.

1. Open a shell window and use su -, and enter the password of the root user.

2. After downloading the installation file, you can find it in the `Downloads` folder of the user account that has downloaded the file. Typically, this is `/home/<username>/Downloads`. Use the `cd` command to go to this directory.

3. The downloaded file has a name that looks like `VMware-Workstation-Full-<version>.bundle`. Use the command bash `VMware-Workstation-Full-<version>.bundle` to start **VMware Workstation Installer**. This launches the graphical installation program. Select **I agree** to indicate that you agree to the license terms and then click on **Next** to continue.

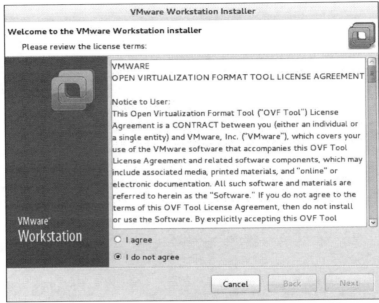

On Linux as well, you'll install VMware Workstation using a graphical installation program

4. The installation program now opens a few windows in which it asks for generic settings. In the first window, you'll indicate if you want to check for product updates on startup and next you will express if you want to help VMware by sending anonymous usage data to VMware.

5. As Linux is a multiuser operating system by default, in the next window you can enter the name of a user account that has been used for connecting to VMware Workstation Server. Normally, the root user account is the only account that has sufficient permissions to do this; but if on your Linux computer you have another account with sufficient permissions, enter the name of the account here and click on **Next** to continue.

6. Now you need to enter the name of the path where the shared virtual machines are stored. Note that the path is uncommon; they will be in `/var/lib/vmware/Shared VMs`. This perfectly complies with Linux standards, but it is not typically a location where you would look for these shared files.

7. In the next window, you'll indicate on which port the VMware Workstation Server is offering its services. By default port `443` is used, but if this port is already in use by a web server, you'll have to choose something else. Typically, anything goes as long as the port number is part of the unprivileged port range, which means that it needs to be above port `1024`. `1443` is fine, for instance.

If the Apache server is already using port 443, you'll need to select another port

8. At this point, the installation program has all the data it needs. Click on **Install** to start the installation procedure.

Starting VMware Workstation for the first time

After installing it, you can start VMware Workstation for the first time. But before you can actually start creating the first virtual machine, there are a few steps that still need to be completed. First, you'll need to accept the license agreement. Once you've done that, you will see the VMware Workstation dashboard in which all of the common tasks that are performed in VMware Workstation are summarized. In the following screenshot, you can see what the dashboard looks like. In the next chapter, you'll learn how to continue and create your first virtual machine.

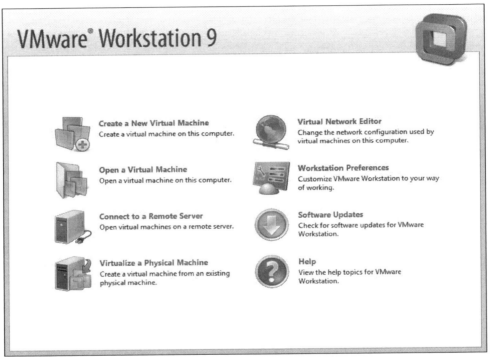

The VMware Workstation dashboard

Before you start creating your first virtual machine, there are a few VMware Workstation settings that you might want to change. To access these settings, either click on **Workstation Preferences** or open the **Edit** menu and select **Preferences**.

The **Preferences** option allows you to set preferences for different features; some of them are self-explanatory. In this section, you'll just read about the most interesting settings. An important feature that you'll find under the **Workspace** option is **Default hardware compatibility**. This option is normally set to the most recent version of VMware Workstation. If, however, you plan on exchanging virtual machines with users of previous versions frequently, you might want to change this to an earlier version. Another important option that you'll find here is ESX Server compatibility. If you plan to upload virtual machines to ESX Server, make sure that **Compatible with ESX Server** is selected. Without this option selected, you won't be able to upload virtual machines to an ESX environment.

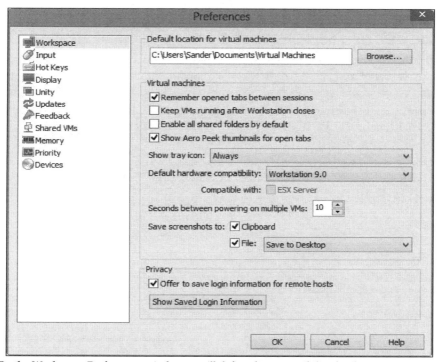

On the Workspace Preferences window, you'll define the compatibility for the VMs you create

To define special key combinations that you can use for commonly used virtual machine operations, you can use the **Hot Keys** tab. On this tab, for instance, you'll define which keys you'll use to release control from a virtual machine and get back to the host environment. By default, the *Ctrl + Alt* keys are used for this purpose. On some operating systems, this key already has a different meaning; on Linux, for instance, you use it to open different virtual consoles. If you want to keep this functionality, you can define another hotkey sequence.

An important part of the configuration of your VMware Workstation host is the amount of RAM that you'll make available for the use of the virtual machines. On one hand, you need to make sure that there is enough RAM remaining to keep the host operating system running smoothly. On the other hand, you also want to make sure that you have enough RAM to allocate the needs of all of your virtual machines. If you don't have sufficient RAM for the host operating system, it will start swapping, and if you don't have enough RAM for the virtual machines, the virtual machine memory will get swapped, neither of which is good for the performance of your computer.

Also under **Memory**, you can specify how the swap is going to be used. The best option for good performance is to disallow the usage of the swap completely. To do this select **Fit all virtual memory into reserved host RAM**, but this means that you might not be able to run all the virtual machines that you need on your host computer. The default option, which is selected, is **Allow some virtual machine memory to be swapped**. This offers the best compromise between performance and the amount of virtual machines that you can run. If you want to be able to run as many virtual machines as possible on the available hardware at the host computer, select **Allow most virtual machine memory to be swapped**; but be prepared for bad performance if you plan to run multiple virtual machines on your computer.

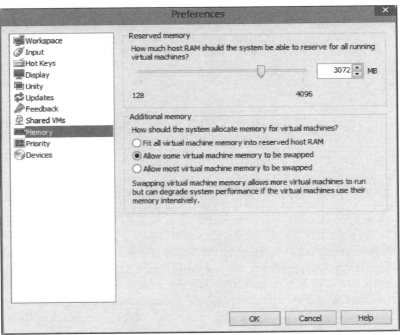

On the Memory tab, you can specify how the host operating system will manage system memory for your virtual machines

On the **Priority** tab, you need to specify that a virtual machine should get extra priority if it is active. By default, there is no additional priority for the virtual machine even if it is active. If you want to speed up the virtual machine a bit while working on it, make sure that **High** is selected on the **Input grabbed** option. To make sure that the host works smoothly while no virtual machines are in use, make sure that the **Input ungrabbed** option reads **Low**.

Another performance-related option specifies how to deal with snapshots. The default options will run the snapshot process in the background irrespective of whether you are taking a snapshot or restoring a snapshot. However, running snapshots in the background ensures that changes are only applied when the virtual machine is off. If you want to apply changes directly, you will need to make sure that the snapshot program runs as a foreground job. This will, however, slow down other processes on your computer as the snapshot process is both heavy in I/O as well as in CPU usage.

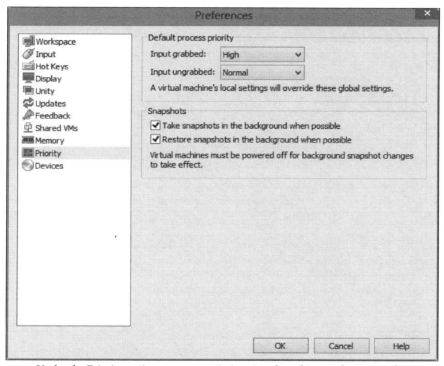

Under the Priority option, you can optimize virtual machine performance a bit

Summary

In this chapter, you have learned how to install VMware Workstation on both Linux and Windows. You have also read about some of the most useful generic program options that you can set.

In the next chapter, you'll learn how to create virtual machines.

2

Installing Virtual Machines

In this chapter, you'll read about how to install virtual machines. As the installation of a basic virtual machine can be very easy, we'll focus on advanced configuration options.

Before you start

Before you start the actual installation of virtual machines, you should set the default location where the virtual machine disk files are going to be stored. If you don't do this, they will get stored in the home directory of the user that uses VMware Workstation. There's nothing wrong with that, but if you're setting up an environment where many virtual machines are going to be used, you probably want to store all virtual machine disk files on a dedicated hard disk. To do this, navigate to **Edit | Preferences** and make sure the **Workspace** option is selected as shown in the following screenshot:

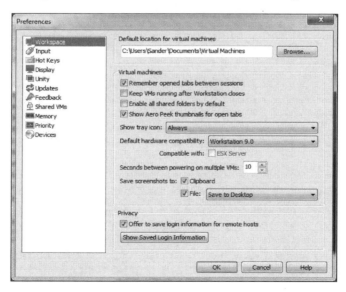

Now browse to the disk and folder where you want to store the virtual machine files. This default location will be applied to all the virtual machines you are going to create from this moment.

Starting the installation

To start the installation of virtual machines, you need to navigate to **File | New Virtual Machine**. This starts **New Virtual Machine Wizard**. The wizard proposes two different options: you can select **Typical** if you want to have your virtual machine up and running as fast as possible, or select **Custom** if you want maximum control over the options that you'll use in the virtual machine. In this procedure, you'll read about how to install a custom virtual machine.

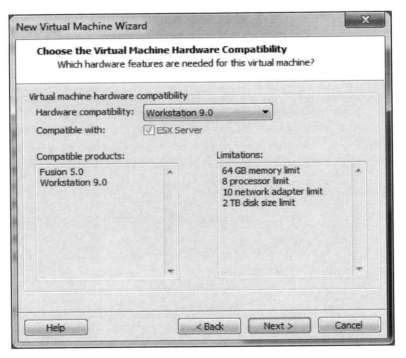

After selecting the custom installation type, you need to specify the virtual machine's hardware compatibility. By default, the VM will install as a VMware Workstation 9 virtual machine type, which is fine if you just want to use it on VMware Workstation 9. However, this VM type won't work on previous versions of VMware Workstation. VMware Workstation 9 uses a new data format that cannot be used on any previous versions of VMware Workstation. For this reason, you can select the lowest version of VMware Workstation that you want the VM to be available on.

Note that you don't have to do anything for compatibility with VMware ESX—the enterprise level virtualization platform. Virtual machines that are compatible with VMware Workstation 6.x or later are automatically fit to run on ESX Server. If you select a compatibility version previous to VMware Workstation 6.x, you need to select ESX Server 5.x or ESX Server 4.x to make sure it will run on ESX.

While selecting the hardware compatibility version, you'll also be able to see which features are supported. On selecting a previous version of VMware Workstation, you'll immediately see which hardware features are unsupported. If, for instance, you select VMware Workstation 4.x, you'll notice that many hardware features are not available and also that the hardware you can use is rather limited with just 3.5 GB of RAM and one CPU.

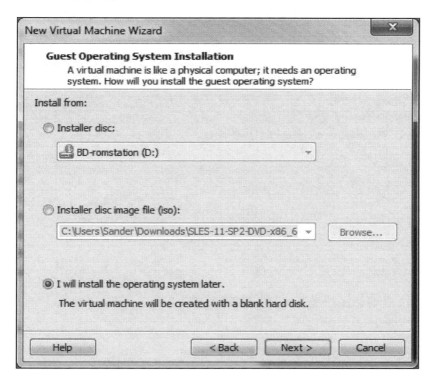

After specifying the hardware compatibility, you can select the installation media you want to use. You can start the installation either from an ISO image file or from a physical disk. Both of these options will launch an easy installation. In this installation type, you will specify a minimal amount of installation options; this means that there will be many choices that won't even be shown by the installation program. Although useful if you just want to get up and running as soon as possible, this kind of installation is not typically the installation that is fit for advanced users. For complete control over the installation processes, it's a good idea to select **I will install the operating system later**.

In the next window, you can indicate which operating system you're going to install. Selecting the operating system automatically sets some of the hardware settings that are needed in the virtual machine. Many different operating systems are supported; the only requirement is that they need to use the same CPU architecture. That is, you can install any Intel-based operating system in VMware Workstation, but it isn't possible to install operating systems that have been written for different hardware architecture, such as IBM System z.

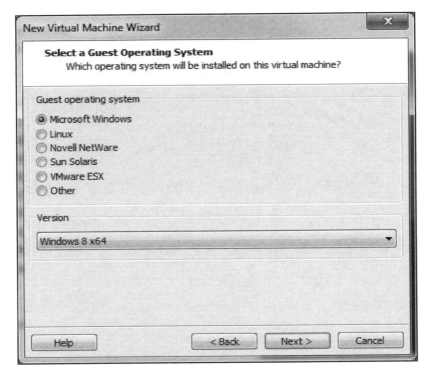

After specifying the operating system, you'll need to select where you want to store the virtual machine disk file. Even if you did already select the default location for virtual machine files, you can still select a different directory for individual virtual machines.

RAM and CPU

In the next window, you'll select the amount of virtual CPUs and the amount of CPU cores that you want available in the virtual machine. Although it might seem tempting to go beyond the number of CPUs that are available in the hardware of your computer, this is not a good idea. For optimal performance in your virtual machine, one CPU with one core will perform best. If you do need multiple CPUs or CPU cores in the virtual machine, you shouldn't go beyond the number of CPUs and cores that are physically available in the host. If you do go beyond this amount, you will notice that the performance of the virtual machines is severely compromised.

The next setting is rather easy: you'll need to select the amount of RAM that is going to be used by the virtual machine. The software allows you to go beyond the amount of RAM that is physically installed on your computer. Avoid this because the virtual machine will eat up all memory on the host and you won't be able to use your computer efficiently anymore.

Networking

After specifying the amount of RAM you want to use, you'll select how to deal with networking. You have four options:

- **Use bridged networking**: Use this option if you want the virtual machine to be directly available on the local network. To use this option, the virtual machine needs a dedicated IP address.

- **Use network address translation (NAT)**: This is the default option for networking. The virtual machine can access other computers on the network, but it won't be accessible by itself as this access is prevented by the NAT firewall.

- **Use host-only networking**: Use this option if you want to set up a test network in which the computers don't need to access anything on external networks.

In *Chapter 3, Working with Virtual Machines,* you'll learn how to set up virtual networking in much more detail. If you're not sure about what to do, select **Use network address translation (NAT)** and continue, as shown in the following screenshot:

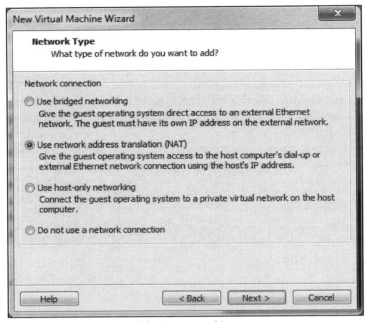

Selecting networking

Disk options

Next, you'll specify which type of **SCSI controller** you want to be used by the virtual machine. By default, this will be an SAS controller, which offers the best performance, but if you know that your virtual machine doesn't support this controller type, you can select a regular **LSI Logic** controller.

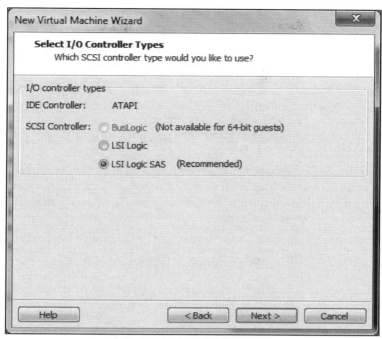

Selecting the SCSI disk controller

Now you'll indicate what type of disk you want to use. By default, VMware will create a disk image file in the location that you specified for this purpose earlier. You can, however, also select an existing disk file or install directly on a physical disk. Using a VMware disk file is the most flexible option as you can easily copy or move the disk to another computer that is using VMware and import it there. For optimum performance, you can use a physical disk. The advantage of this is that VMware doesn't have to go through a filesystem layer to access files that are on a physical disk and that makes it faster. However, it also makes your setup less flexible because physical disks are not easy to resize.

 If you want to use physical disks as the storage backend of your virtual machines, consider using a Linux host operating system. On Linux, you can use LVM, which is a flexible way of addressing disk storage. In LVM, it becomes easy to resize the disk; this can be seen in VMware.

The option to use an existing disk is not something that you would use to create a new virtual machine, but to import an existing virtual machine that was made on another computer. In *Chapter 6, Accessing Virtual Machines Remotely*, you'll learn how to import virtual machines.

After selecting what kind of disk you want to use, you need to select the disk type as well. You can choose between SCSI and IDE. For optimal performance, SCSI is the preferred disk type. Only if you want to work with a legacy operating system such as MS-DOS does it makes sense to select an IDE disk.

Next, you'll need to specify how you want to allocate disk space. VMware Workstation uses thin provisioning by default. This means that you'll need to specify the maximum amount of space that the disk can use, but not all of this disk space will be allocated immediately. If you want to use a minimum amount of available disk space to set up your virtual machines, this is a good option. If, however, you want the best possible performance, it's not so good. For maximum performance, better select **Allocate all disk space now**. This will create the virtual disk before starting the installation of the virtual machine—note that this may take a considerable amount of time.

You can also specify if you want to use either one disk file or multiple disk files. By default, VMware Workstation uses multiple disk files; this makes it easier to copy the files elsewhere. An important reason to do this is that some file systems don't support large disk files. For optimal performance, however, it is better to use one disk file only.

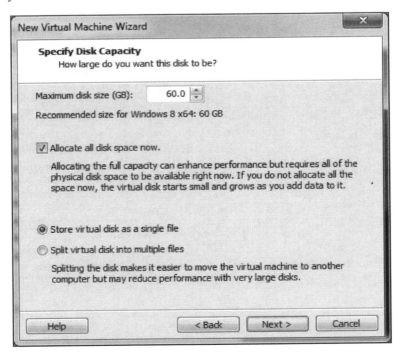

After specifying how the disk file must be created, you'll indicate the name of the disk file. By default, the name of the disk files is the same as the name of the virtual machine. The file uses the default extension .vmdk.

At this point, you have specified all that VMware needs to know to start the installation of your virtual machine. You'll now see an overview window from which you can customize the hardware. Once you've done that, click on **Finish** to close the installer window. This will define the VMware machine. If you have selected to install later, the configuration will be written to the disk, after which you can start the installation.

Installing a Windows 8 virtual machine

In the previous section, you read about how to specify hardware settings for the virtual machines you want to install. Based on this, you can now install a virtual machine. In this section, you'll read about how to install a Windows 8 virtual machine.

In the previous procedure, you have read about how to define the hardware settings for the virtual machine you want to create. After the hardware options have been defined, the virtual machine is added to the VMware dashboard. Before you can start the actual installation, you'll now first have to define the installation disk that you want to use. To do this, select **Virtual Machine** from the VMware dashboard and click on **Edit virtual machine settings**.

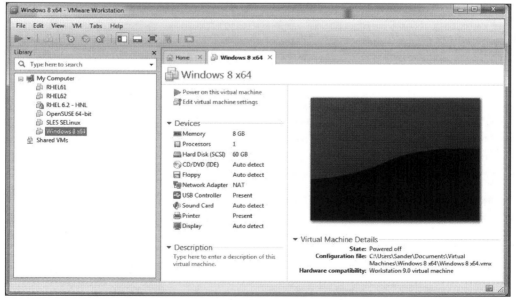

Click on Edit virtual machine settings to specify the installation medium

After clicking on **Edit virtual machine settings**, on the **Hardware** tab select **CD/DVD (IDE)**. If you want to install from an ISO file, click on **Use ISO image file** and browse to the file you want to use to start the installation.

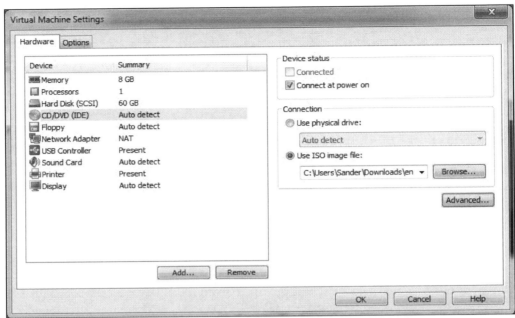

Select the ISO file you want to use for the installation

Now click on the **OK** button to save the settings and click on the **Play** button to start the virtual machine. You'll now see the virtual machine starting, with the virtual machine startup windows shown in a window within the VMware Workstation console. In case the installation program doesn't fit, you can maximize this window. The easiest way to do this is using the buttons on top of the installer window. Hover the mouse over the buttons to see a description of each; you need to enter fullscreen mode to work conveniently from a fullscreen environment. To get back out of the fullscreen display, use the *Ctrl + Alt* keys simultaneously. Next, move the mouse button to the upper part of the screen to show the button bar. You can see that the fullscreen button is currently active; click on it again to deactivate it.

The installation procedure itself is the same as the way that you are familiar with it on a normal Windows installation. Complete all of the required steps to finish the installation. Note that you do need a valid registration key to install Windows 8. If you want to set up a Windows 8 machine for testing purposes, you can request an evaluation key from www.microsoft.com. Even if it is just for testing purposes, you will need to register the virtual machine at www.microsoft.com; it is not possible to complete the installation procedure without registration.

Installing a Linux virtual machine

Installing a Windows virtual machine is easy as Windows integrates very well in VMware. Installing a Linux virtual machine is a bit more difficult because you'll need to install the VMware Tools in the Linux operating system. In the following procedure, you can read about how to handle the VMware-specific parts of the installation on a Linux virtual machine.

The beginning of the installation procedure for a Linux virtual machine is very similar to the installation of a Windows virtual machine. With Linux, it is even more important to select the option **I will install the operating system later** to avoid an easy install. This is because Linux has so many options that can be modified to match the needs of the user, and if you use an easy install, all you get is default values.

Some Linux distributions don't show the graphical display as they should. To fix this, stop the installation and navigate to **Virtual Machine Settings | Hardware**. From there, navigate to **Display | Specify monitor settings** and manually set the display resolution you want to use. You can now restart the installation.

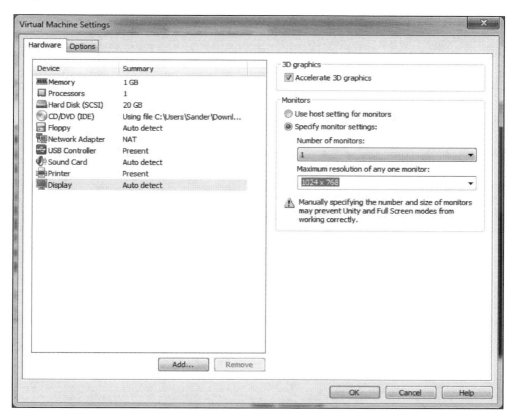

Once the installation program has loaded, continue the installation as normal. While selecting the software you want to install, make sure to install the kernel-source package, as well as the GCC compiler, and get all the related tools. This will make installing VMware Tools a lot easier. Once completed, click on **I Finished Installing** in the lower part of the installation window.

The difficult part of installing a Linux virtual machine is to get VMware Tools in the virtual machine. VMware Tools ensures that the appropriate drivers for graphics, network, and disk are installed. Using VMware Tools really makes the performance of the virtual machine a lot better, but installing the tools in Linux is a bit difficult. The difficulty is that to install VMware Tools, you will need to mount an ISO of the VMware Tools image in the virtual machine. The VMware Tools installation files are copied from the image file to the disk in the virtual machine, but in order to do this, you'll need access to the installation disk on most Linux distributions at the same time.

Repositories

To install VMware Tools, additional software has to be copied from the installation sources, the so-called repositories, your Linux distribution uses. If you have registered your Linux VM online, you will use online repositories, so the only condition is that you need to have an active Internet connection. If your Linux distribution is not actually online, you need to make the installation files available locally. The easiest way to do this is to copy the installation image to the virtual machine and configure that as a repository. Consult the documentation for your distribution, as the exact procedure to be applied is different for each distribution.

To install VMware Tools, you first have to disconnect the installation disk. To do this, click on the CD icon in the lower right part of the screen and click on **Disconnect** (see the following screenshot).

Before installing VMware Tools, disconnect the installation disk

After disconnecting the installation disk, in VMware Workstation open the VM menu and select **Install VMware tools**. This mounts the VMware Tools image in the guest operating system. Now open a root shell in the Linux virtual machine and type the mount command to find out where the VMware Tools disk has been mounted to. On a modern Fedora system, for instance, it will be mounted on `/run/media/user`. Use `cd` to go to the mount point of the CD-ROM in this directory.

Manually mounting the Tools image

If you can't find the VMware Tools image mounted anywhere, you can mount it manually. To do this, open a root terminal and use the command mount `/dev/sr0 /mnt`.

Once you've accessed the directory where the VMware Tools image is mounted, use `cp` to copy the installation file to the `/tmp` directory. For instance, use `cp VMware[Tab] /tmp` to copy the tools file. Next, enter the following commands to extract the tools file:

```
cd /tmp
tar zvf VMware[Tab]
```

You'll now have a directory `/tmp/vmware-tools-distrib` that contains the installation files for VMware Tools. Use `cd` to enter that directory and next enter the `./vmware-install.pl` command to start the tools installation. This starts the interactive installation program. Press *Enter* to accept all the default answers to the questions that are asked at this moment. If you encounter error messages, follow the directions of the installation program to fix the errors. Once completely installed, the easiest way to activate the newly installed VMware Tools is to restart your Linux virtual machine.

Summary

In this chapter, you have read about how to install virtual machines. The chapter started with an explanation of the virtual hardware that is used for the virtual machines; after this, you read about how to install a Windows virtual machine as well as a Linux virtual machine. In the next chapter, you'll read about the basics of virtual machine usage.

3
Working with Virtual Machines

In many ways, working with virtual machines is like working with physical machines. In some aspects, there are important differences. In this chapter, you'll learn about these differences that can sometimes make working with virtual machines a bit of a challenge. In this chapter, you'll also learn how to deal with the various particularities of working in a virtual environment.

Performing common tasks

Even the most common tasks can be different in a virtual machine. It starts with the virtual machine window itself. Once you're on it, the mouse cursor is captured. That means you'll need to apply a special trick to get back to the host operating system. The common way to do this is by pressing *Ctrl + Alt* at the same time. But what if in the virtual operating system, the *Ctrl + Alt* keys sequence has a specific meaning? If that's the case, you'll need to define the hot keys that are used in your virtual environment. To do this, apply the following procedure:

1. From the **Edit** menu, select the **Preferences** option.

2. In the bar on the left of the screen, select **Hot Keys**.

3. You'll now see the interface that is shown in the following screenshot. By default, the *Ctrl + Alt* keys are used as the virtual machine hotkeys, and specific manipulations are assigned to these hotkeys.

4. Click on the hotkeys that you want to be redefined. For instance, if you want to use *Shift* + **Win** as the default hotkeys, click on these buttons:

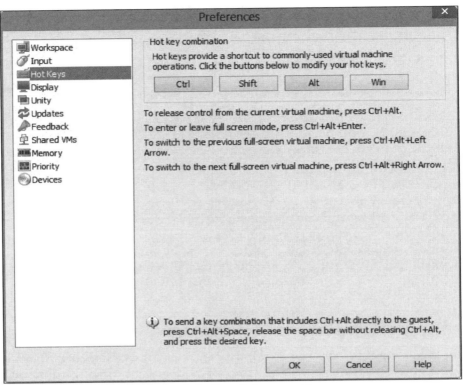

Assigning the hotkeys that you want to use

 Don't forget to deselect the hotkeys that you don't want to use anymore; you probably don't want to use key sequences such as *Ctrl* + *Shift* + *Alt* + **Win** all at the same time!

Now that you have assigned the hotkeys that make sense to you, you can use them for some of the most common actions:

- Use the hotkeys to release control from the current machine
- Use the hotkeys + *Enter* to enter or leave the fullscreen mode
- Use hotkeys + left arrow or right arrow to switch to the previous or the next virtual machine

Another common task is about **Updates**. You can access this feature from the **Preferences** menu as well. By default, VMware Workstation will check for updates on startup, and it will automatically update software components that you're using as well. That's just fine and there is no reason why you would want to change that.

A very useful update option that is not enabled by default is the update of VMware Tools. By default, the VMware Tools that are installed in a virtual machine are never updated. If you want the best possible performance for your virtual machine, it does make sense to update VMware Tools automatically as well. You should realize that using the latest version of VMware Tools ensures the best possible performance, especially on I/O-drivers. To do this select the **Updates** option from the **Preferences** tab and select **Automatically update VMware Tools on a virtual machine**.

Working with hardware

Each virtual machine has hardware assigned. You have selected the hardware that you want to use while creating the virtual machine. On an installed virtual machine, you will frequently modify hardware settings as well. On some occasions, it will be necessary to assign a new virtual hardware but common tasks such as booting from a CD-ROM requires some specific action as well.

Booting your virtual machine from a CD-ROM

There are different ways to boot a virtual machine. You can either use a physical CD-ROM or a DVD disk or as an alternative, you can boot from an ISO file. Using ISO files is useful, as you don't have to make sure the physical disk is present for all operations you want to perform.

To tell your virtual machine where it needs to boot from, boot into **BIOS** to change the boot order. To enter the **BIOS** setup for the guest operating system, navigate to **VM | Power | Power On to BIOS**.

 To make the boot delay a bit longer, you can add the following to the VMX file of your virtual machine: `bios.bootDelay = 1000`. This will give you 3 seconds of time to interfere with the boot process.

Booting a virtual machine from a CD-ROM can be a real challenge. This is because you'll have a minimal amount of time to press the right key to boot from an optical disk while the virtual machine is booting, and also you need to make sure that you are connected to the right virtual CD-ROM. In the following procedure, you can read how it works:

1. Restart your virtual machine.

2. When you see the virtual machine **BIOS** loading, immediately click on the virtual machine window and press the *Esc* key. This will show the **BIOS** menu (see the following screenshot):

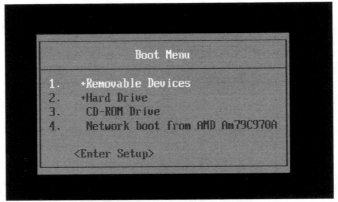

The virtual machine's BIOS boot menu

3. Don't select CD-ROM from the virtual machine **BIOS** yet but open the **VM** menu, navigate to **Removable Devices | CD/DVD**, and click on **Settings**. This opens the virtual machine's hardware settings window with **CD/DVD** selected. Make sure that you've selected either the correct physical drive that contains the CD-ROM disk that you want to use or use an image file to select an ISO image file.

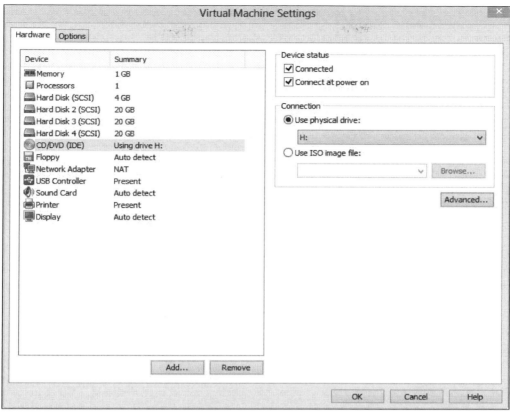

Selecting the CD-ROM disk you want to use

4. Click on **OK** to save the selected optical disk.

5. Get back to **BIOS Boot Menu** of your virtual machine and select **CD-ROM Drive**. The virtual machine will now boot from the CD-ROM disk.

Modifying virtual hardware

When you created your virtual machine, you also selected the hardware that you want to use. One of the benefits of working with virtual machines is that it is easy to change the hardware settings later if needed. To access the current hardware settings, right-click on **virtual machine** and select the **Settings** option. From here, you can see all the hardware that is currently selected and change the hardware assignments as well. If VMware Tools are installed, some setting will even be applied directly to the virtual machine without the need to reboot it.

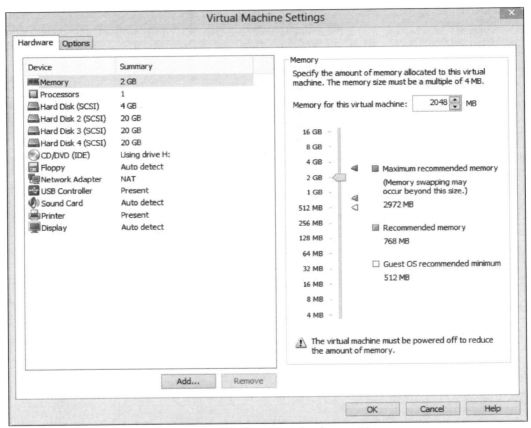

Changing the virtual machine's hardware settings

While adding virtual hardware, in most cases, you can be very specific about the properties of the hardware that is added. In the following procedure, you'll read how to add a disk and configure some advanced disk properties. Especially when setting up test environments that need to mirror the production environment, it can be important to specify properties such as the SCSI ID or disk type.

1. Right-click on the virtual machine to which you want to add a new disk and open the **Settings** menu item. In this example, I'll add a disk to a Linux VM.

2. Click on **Add** and from the **Hardware Type** window, select **Hard Disk**.

3. Select **Create a new virtual disk** and click on **Next**.

4. At this point, you can specify whether you want the disk to be an independent disk or not. This is an important choice with regard to snapshots; independent disks are not affected by snapshots (discussed in detail in *Chapter 8, Cloning and Snapshots*, of this book). When you make a snapshot of a disk, the disk needs to be stopped for a short moment. For some services (such as databases), you really don't want a disk to be stopped even if it is just for a short moment. In those cases, it makes sense to configure the disk as an independent disk, but be aware that you won't be able to create a snapshot of such a disk.

5. When creating an independent disk, you need to specify how changes are handled. The default behavior is to write them directly to the disk. Another option is to make the changes nonpersistent, which means that you will lose them if you power off the virtual machine.

6. After specifying which type of disk you want to use, you need to configure the disk capacity. An important part of the configuration is whether or not you want to allocate all disk space now. By default, thin provisioning is used, which means that the disk space is only allocated at the moment when it is actually needed. Thin provisioning means that the available disk space on the host operating system is used as efficiently as possible but there is a performance penalty. If the available disk space on the host is not important, and performance is, you had better select the **Allocate all disk space now** option. With this option, you will make sure that all disk space is reserved, which offers best performance for your VM. You also need to specify whether you want the disk to be created as a single file or as multiple files. Using multiple files makes it easier to move a virtual machine to another computer, especially if the FAT32 file system is used on that computer, which has a limited maximal file size. On large disks, you will however pay a performance price when working with multiple files.

7. After specifying the name of the disk file, the file is created and written to the disk. After creating it, you can click on the **Advanced** button to specify some of its properties. In some cases, the order in which the disk is presented to the virtual machine can be important. You can specify this order by selecting the **SCSI** ID. If you want a disk to be presented as the first disk in the virtual operating system (which ensures that it is the bootable device), make sure to configure it as SCSI 0:0 and click on **OK**.

 Changing the order in which disks are presented can have the result that the virtual machine won't boot anymore. Make sure that you know what you're doing before selecting this option.

8. After clicking on **OK,** the new hardware settings are written to the virtual machine. This doesn't activate the new hardware immediately though. On Linux, after adding a SCSI disk, you can tell Linux to reread its disks, which will make the new device available immediately. After adding the new disk as the user root, use the following command to make the new disk available without having to reboot the VM:

```
echo "- - -" > /sys/class/scsi_host/host0/scan
```

Working with shared folders

A very useful feature in VMware Workstation is shared folders. Using shared folders allows you to easily share files between the host operating system and VMware Workstation. Using shared folders allows you to get access to a shared folder on the host computer in the virtual machine.

To work with shared folders, you need to enable them in the virtual machine. Once enabled, you can access them from the virtual machine's operating system. In the following procedure, you can read how it works:

1. Working with shared folders starts on the virtual machine where you want to use it. So make sure that the virtual machine where you want to use it is started.

2. Once the virtual machine is started, select **Settings** from the **VM** menu and click on the **Options** tab. From this tab, select the **Shared Folders** item.

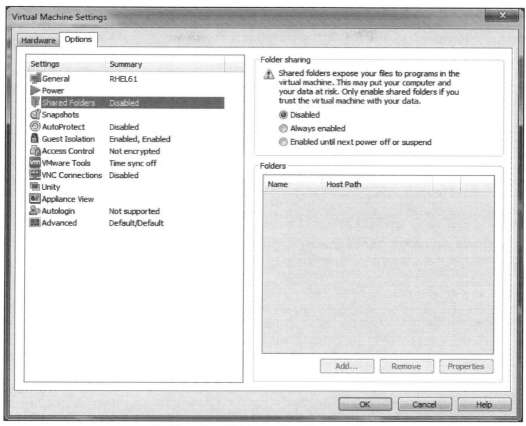

Enabling shared folders on the virtual machine

3. To enable shared folders, you can select **Always enabled** or **Enabled until next power off or suspend**. If you're just looking for an easy way to exchange files, the latter method works best. If you want the files on the shared folder to be always accessible, select **Always enabled**. If you're enabling shared folders for Windows guests, you can indicate that you want to see the shared folder as a network drive in Windows guests.

4. After specifying how you want to use shared folders, click on **Add** to start the **Shared Folder** wizard. In the first step of this wizard, you'll need to select a path on the host computer. Use the **Browse** button to select the appropriate path and give it a name.

5. Next, you'll specify how to share this folder. Click on **Enable this share** for access in full read/write mode, or **Read-only** if you just want to allow files to be read. Next click on **OK**. The shared folder will now be available in the virtual machine.

6. To access a shared folder from a Linux virtual machine, go to the `/mnt/hgfs` directory. The shared folder is mounted there by default. On a Windows virtual machine, you can map a network drive to access the shared folder.

Setting virtual machine options

You've just worked with the virtual machine options item to enable shared folders. There are some other settings that you can select from this tab. Some of the most interesting options are discussed in this section.

Automatic snapshots

When working with a virtual machine, you can have a snapshot created automatically. A snapshot is like a picture of the current state of a virtual machine that allows you to go back to that specific state in an easy way. As an additional protection for virtual machines, you can have snapshots created automatically when powering off. However, using snapshots may be dangerous if you don't know what you're doing; they do use disk space and by using snapshots, you risk running out of available disk space. Also, performance will worsen if there are snapshots for your virtual machines.

To enable the automatic snapshot feature, access the **Snapshots** menu option and select between the following when powering off the options:

*   **Just power off**
*   **Revert to snapshot**
*   **Take a new snapshot**
*   **Ask me**

Notice that the **Revert to snapshot** option is a potentially dangerous option; it will reset your virtual machine to the state it was in when the last snapshot was created, and you will lose all the changes that you've made since.

The **AutoProtect** feature that you can also find in the virtual machine's **Options** menu is related to snapshots. You can use this feature to automatically create snapshots according to the parameters that you've specified. This is a useful feature that always allows you to get back to a reasonably recent state of the virtual machine.

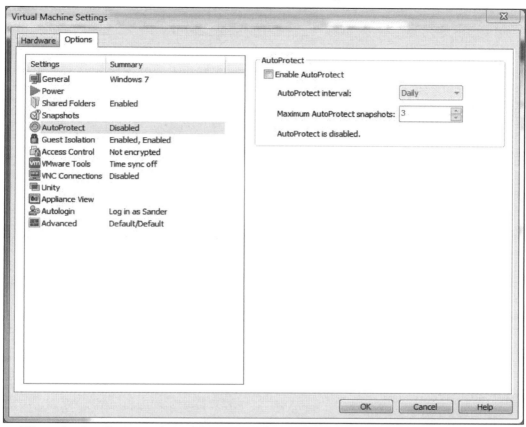

When using AutoProtect, you're sure that you can always revert to a recent state of the virtual machine

Time synchronization

In virtualized environments, time keeping may be a problem. This is because time is based on CPU ticks, and in a VMware Workstation virtual environment, virtual machines don't use CPU ticks the way normal computers do. Therefore, you might see huge time drifting if you don't take the appropriate measures. At the other end, time synchronization is essential because many services rely on the appropriate time.

On the VMware Tools menu option, you'll find an interesting option as well. This option specifies whether you want to use time synchronization or not. By default, the virtual machine doesn't synchronize time with the host. Because of virtual machine's inherent features, this may lead to a time that significantly differs from the real time. To avoid issues, it is a good idea to have the virtual machine synchronize time with the host and to configure NTP time synchronization on the host, which ensures that a reliable time is used on the host as well.

VNC connections

To access a virtual machine, you can configure remote access within the Virtual Machine itself. If, however, you're looking for a more standard method of enabling remote access which works for all virtual machines, no matter which operating system you're using, VNC connections is an interesting option. With VNC, you'll share access from the VMware Workstation host to the entire virtual machine screen. The benefit of this approach is that you can use it to access all virtual machines no matter what operating system is running inside. There is an inconvenience to using VNC though; data that is sent over a VNC connection is not encrypted by default. This means you should only use it to access virtual machines that are on a network connection which you trust completely.

To enable a VNC access to virtual machines, you need to select the Enable VNC connections option on each virtual machine (VM) where you want to use it. Next, you'll need to specify a VNC Port. Every VNC connection will use its own port, so you might end up with one VNC process that is listening on several ports on your host and that is fine. It's also a very good idea to protect each VNC session with a password. If you don't use a password, anyone can just connect to the active sessions on the virtual machine and that is a huge threat to security!

After setting up VNC for virtual machines, you'll need to make sure that you have a VNC client on the remote computer. Different VNC clients are available for free, and you can find one on, for instance, www.realvnc.com.

Securing virtual machines

While using VNC means that you'll weaken security on the virtual machines, you can also choose to add some extra protection. You'll find related options on the **Options** tab of each virtual machine (navigate to **VM | Settings | Options**). The name of the related option is **Access Control**, and you can use it to set different kinds of protection.

First, you can encrypt the virtual machine. This process is equivalent to the encryption of an entire hard disk and if you use it, the virtual machine's disk file won't be accessible without entering the appropriate password. Using this option is recommended if you want to make sure that you can trust the virtual machine in an environment where you cannot be sure whether you can trust the host on which it's running. To enable encryption on a virtual machine, you must first shut down the virtual machine before starting the encryption process. Be aware that it may take a long time for the encryption process to complete, depending on the size of the hard disk where you're applying it to.

After encrypting a virtual machine, you can either remove the encryption or change the encryption password. To do this, first make sure that the virtual machine is powered off; you'll now see the **Change Password** option and the **Remove Encryption** option under **Access Control**.

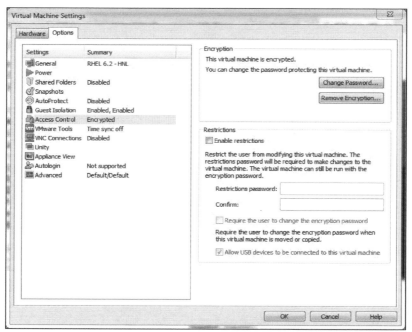

Use encryption if you want to prevent unauthorized access to the virtual machine

On using **Encryption,** just the contents of the virtual machine are encrypted. Users will still be allowed to change the virtual machine's configuration. If you want to prevent this, you should use restrictions as well. After selecting **Enable restrictions,** each user who wants to change the configuration of a virtual machine must first enter **Restrictions password.**

As related options, you can also enforce that the encryption password must be used after moving it. This is a good approach to ensure the security of the passwords that you're using; a password loses its strength if it's used on multiple locations. Also from the **Access Control** tab, you can find an option to disallow USB keys to connect to the virtual machine. By applying all of these options, you'll be able to add a reasonable level of security to your virtual machines.

Summary

In this chapter, you've learned how to work with virtual machines. Different tasks have been discussed, from connecting virtual hardware to changing settings that relate to the security and remote access of virtual machines. In the next chapter, you'll learn what's going on behind the scenes, and the configuration of virtual machines as it exists on the host operating system is discussed in more detail.

4
VMware Workstation behind the Scenes

In the previous chapters, you have learned how to install and use VMware Workstation. In this chapter, you'll take a look behind the scenes and see what has happened on the VMware host computer while the virtual machines were being created. You'll have a look at the configuration files that have been created and the associated disk files. You'll also learn what you need to do when moving VMware disk files to other computers. Also, we'll discuss the different kinds of storage that you can use in a VMware Workstation environment.

Understanding VMware Workstation files

You will change most of the configuration parameters that your virtual machines are using by hand. However, there are situations where it can be very useful to understand the files that are used behind the virtual machine. A few different file types are used as follows:

- VMware Workstation program files
- VMware Workstation virtual machine definition files
- VMware Workstation disk files

In the following sections, these different files will be discussed.

VMware Workstation program files and services

After the installation of VMware Workstation, some program files get copied to your computer. Also, the host computer runs some services that allow you to use VMware Workstation and associated services such as networking. This section gives an overview of the most important program files and services.

Program files on Windows hosts

Most times, you won't do much with the VMware Workstation program files that you find at `directory \Program Files (x86)\VMware \VMware Workstation on a Windows host`. In this directory, you'll find the different binaries that make up VMware Workstation as well as the ISO files that are used in virtual machines when you're installing VMware Tools.

Some helper programs have also been installed in this directory; these include the following:

- `vmware`: This is the VMware Workstation binary. This is the program that you'll launch to get access to VMware Workstation.

- `vmplayer`: This is the free "light" version of VMware Workstation. You'll miss some of the advanced features, but it does allow you to create and run virtual machines.

- `vmnetconfig`: This is the tool that is used to create networks in VMware. You'll read more about this in *Chapter 5, Networking VMware Workstation*, of this book.

Program files on Linux hosts

If you're using VMware Workstation on Linux, there are many more utilities that you can use. To get an overview of all of them, open a Linux root shell prompt and type `vmware[Tab] [Tab]`. This gives you an overview of all the VMware utilities that are available.

Showing VMware management utilities on Linux

A list of all the useful VMware command-line utilities and a short description of what you can do with the command is as follows:

- `vmware-hostd`: This command interfaces with the VMware service that runs on your Linux machine. Use this command to automatically start all virtual machines that should be started automatically (`-a`) or to automatically upgrade all legacy virtual machines.

- `vmware-mount`: This is a very useful command that helps you mount virtual disk image files and get information directly out of the virtual disk. This command is helpful if for some reason you cannot start the related virtual machine anymore.

- `vmware-networks`: This command is used to manage VMware networks from the command line. In *Chapter 5, Networking VMware Workstation*, which covers networking in detail, you can read more about using this command.

- `vmware-usbarbitrator`: This command helps you analyze the way that USB keys are managed in a VMware environment. Use this command to troubleshoot USB keys that won't work in a virtual machine. Particularly useful is the (`-info`) option that shows log messages about USB keys that are attached to the host and the virtual machines that are used on it.

- `vmware-vdiskmanaager`: This command-line utility allows you to manage VMware virtual disks outside of a virtual machine. Later in this chapter, you can read about how to use this command to manipulate virtual disk properties.

VMware services

After the installation of VMware Workstation, the host computer will also run several VMware services. An overview and short description of all the services is as follows:

- **VMware-hostd service**: This is the VMware Workstation service. It allows VMware Workstation to run on your computer and also makes it possible to establish remote connections to your instance of VMware Workstation.

- **VMware Authorization Service**: This service helps virtual machines get the appropriate permissions to the host operating system. If the service isn't running, virtual machines will complain about that when they're starting up. If the service is running, you'll be fine.

- **VMware NAT Service**: This service is used in the VMware network to make virtual machines reachable over NAT. Make sure it is running if you're using virtual networks with NAT.

- **VMware USB Arbitration Service**: USB devices cannot be used in the virtual machine and on the host operating system simultaneously. That is why the VMware USB Arbitration Service is used; it makes sure that a USB device is available either in the virtual machine or in the host, but not in both at the same time.

- **VMware VMnet DHCP Service**: This service runs DHCP on the virtual network. Make sure it is running if your virtual machines are configured to get an IP address from a DHCP service.

Working with VMware Workstation files

After a virtual machine has been installed, different files are copied to the host computer. On Linux, by default these files are stored in the folder vmware that is created in the home folder of the user who creates the files. On Windows, a folder with the name Virtual Machines is created in the Documents folder. This folder contains the complete virtual machine configuration.

The main configuration file of the virtual machine is in the .vmx file. Associated with that is a .vmxf file in which the version of virtual hardware used is listed. Then there is the .log file containing log messages related to the virtual machine, and as the last part of the virtual machine files, there are the .vmdk files that are used as a virtual disk in the virtual machine. Associated files will be present as well; these are used to represent the current state of a virtual machine and they are not as important as the other files.

One file type that might be relevant however is the .lck file. This is the lock file that indicates that a virtual machine is in use. On some occasions, after the shutdown of a virtual machine, it may happen that the lock file is not properly removed. If this is the case (which shows clearly as the machine will refuse to boot, complaining about the .lck file), you can remove the .lck files to enable the startup of the virtual machine again.

VMware Workstation virtual machine definition files

For every virtual machine that you create, a .vmx file is created. The settings of the virtual machine are stored in this file, and on some occasions, you'll have to change the settings in the .vmx file as they won't be available in the graphical management interface. In the following code listing, you can see the .vmx file of a virtual machine that was created on a Linux host (for better readability, some lines have been removed):

```
vmwarehost:/home/user/vmware/OpenSUSE 64-bit # cat OpenSUSE\ 64-
   bit.vmx
#!/usr/bin/vmware
.encoding = "UTF-8"
config.version = "8"
virtualHW.version = "9"
vcpu.hotadd = "TRUE"
scsi0.present = "TRUE"
scsi0.virtualDev = "lsilogic"
memsize = "768"
mem.hotadd = "TRUE"
scsi0:0.present = "TRUE"
scsi0:0.fileName = "OpenSUSE 64-bit.vmdk"
ide0:0.present = "TRUE"
ide0:0.fileName = "auto detect"
ide0:0.deviceType = "cdrom-raw"
ethernet0.present = "TRUE"
ethernet0.connectionType = "nat"
ethernet0.virtualDev = "e1000"
ethernet0.wakeOnPcktRcv = "FALSE"
ethernet0.addressType = "generated"
usb.present = "TRUE"
ehci.present = "TRUE"
ehci.pciSlotNumber = "35"
sound.present = "TRUE"
sound.startConnected = "FALSE"
sound.fileName = "-1"
sound.autodetect = "TRUE"
usb.vbluetooth.startConnected = "TRUE"
displayName = "OpenSUSE 64-bit"
guestOS = "opensuse-64"
nvram = "OpenSUSE 64-bit.nvram"
scsi0.pciSlotNumber = "16"
ethernet0.generatedAddress = "00:0c:29:f6:5e:ae"
```

```
ethernet0.pciSlotNumber = "33"
ethernet0.generatedAddressOffset = "0"
tools.remindInstall = "FALSE"
vmotion.checkpointFBSize = "134217728"
softPowerOff = "FALSE"
usb:0.deviceType = "hid"
usb:0.port = "0"
usb:0.parent = "-1"
usb:1.speed = "2"
usb:1.deviceType = "hub"
usb:1.port = "1"
usb:1.parent = "-1"
vmx.onpoweronkeys = "1"
floppy0.autodetect = "TRUE"
vmx.onpoweron0.key = "ide0:0.present"
vmx.onpoweron0.value = "FALSE"
ide0:0.autodetect = "TRUE"
ide1:0.autodetect = "TRUE"
vmwarehost:/home/user/vmware/OpenSUSE 64-bit #
```

As you can see, the entire configuration of the virtual machine is specified in the .vmx file. You can also see that it includes some hardware settings that are not easily accessible from the VMware graphical management interface. You can change settings in this file using an editor as long as you make sure that you use the correct syntax.

An example of a situation when you might want to change the .vmx file's contents is after copying a virtual machine to another host. If you do this, the same MAC address will be used on the other host. To change the MAC address, just open the .vmx file in an editor and select the value for the ethernet0.generatedAddress parameter. If you do so, make sure though that the virtual machine is not currently running, or else the settings will be overwritten when you shut down the virtual machines.

VMware Workstation disk files

In VMware Workstation, files are used to represent disks in the virtual machine by default. You can find these files in the virtual machine directory and easily recognize them by the .vmdk extension.

By default, when creating a virtual machine, several disk files are created. For virtual machines that use large disks, you may find dozens of disk files. This is to ensure that the virtual machine files can be used on any filesystem, even limited filesystems such as FAT32, where the maximal disk size is limited. As discussed before, if you know beforehand that the virtual machines will never be used on a limited filesystem, you're better off creating one big disk file per virtual machine.

When loading the disk of a virtual machine that uses many virtual machine disk files, the .vmdk file that doesn't include a number (such as s0001.vmdk) is read first. This file contains a list of all the other .vmdk files that the virtual machine uses, and some other metadata as well. The following code listing shows a part of the contents of the master .vmdk file:

```
vmwarehost:/home/user/vmware/OpenSUSE 64-bit # cat OpenSUSE\ 64-bit.
vmdk
# Disk DescriptorFile
version=1
encoding="UTF-8"
CID=bb3b482f
parentCID=ffffffff
isNativeSnapshot="no"
createType="twoGbMaxExtentSparse"

# Extent description
RW 4192256 SPARSE "OpenSUSE 64-bit-s001.vmdk"
RW 4192256 SPARSE "OpenSUSE 64-bit-s002.vmdk"
RW 4192256 SPARSE "OpenSUSE 64-bit-s003.vmdk"
RW 4192256 SPARSE "OpenSUSE 64-bit-s004.vmdk"
RW 4192256 SPARSE "OpenSUSE 64-bit-s005.vmdk"
RW 4192256 SPARSE "OpenSUSE 64-bit-s006.vmdk"
RW 4192256 SPARSE "OpenSUSE 64-bit-s007.vmdk"
RW 4192256 SPARSE "OpenSUSE 64-bit-s008.vmdk"
RW 4192256 SPARSE "OpenSUSE 64-bit-s009.vmdk"
RW 4192256 SPARSE "OpenSUSE 64-bit-s010.vmdk"
RW 20480 SPARSE "OpenSUSE 64-bit-s011.vmdk"

# The Disk Data Base
#DDB

ddb.toolsVersion = "9282"
ddb.adapterType = "lsilogic"
ddb.geometry.sectors = "63"
ddb.geometry.heads = "255"
ddb.geometry.cylinders = "2610"
ddb.uuid = "60 00 C2 97 7d 00 44 2b-53 6d e1 38 f2 fd fc 4b"
ddb.longContentID = "454b171cf307254b174a0264bb3b482f"
ddb.virtualHWVersion = "9"
vmwarehost:/home/user/vmware/OpenSUSE 64-bit #
```

As you can see, the disk geometry is included in the master .vmdk file as well; this makes it possible for any tool that understands VMDK files to read the contents of the disk file and access its data. This is useful in a migration scenario where you might want to import a VMware-created virtual machine to some other virtualization platform.

Configuring advanced storage

In VMware Workstation virtual machines, you have lots of options to work with virtual machine disks. Some of the most common advanced scenarios will be discussed in the following sections. You'll read about using raw devices as disks in a virtual machine, mounting virtual machine disk files from a Linux host operating system, and changing some properties of virtual disks.

Using devices as virtual machine disks

When a virtual machine is being created, the virtual machine will use a virtual machine disk file by default. In some situations, it may be preferable to use a raw device instead of a virtual machine disk file, particularly if the performance matters. As VMware Workstation always uses a filesystem on a host operating system, some delay will be caused as a result of this. When the virtual machine writes directly on a raw device, this delay is avoided. But using a raw device means that you will need to prepare this device before starting the installation.

If you're using Windows as the host operating system, it means that you'll need to prepare the hard disk of the host in a way that unallocated disk space is available after the installation of the host operating system. Alternatively, you could connect a new dedicated disk to the host computer and use that as a disk in the virtual machine.

If you're using Linux as the host operating system, you can use Logical Volumes (LVM). On an LVM-based Linux system, it is relatively easy to create an LVM logical volume for each virtual machine. Consult the Linux documentation for advice on how to create LVM logical volumes; an in-depth discussion on LVM is beyond the scope of this book.

Before starting to work on raw devices as the storage backend for VM disk files, you should realize that you'll lose flexibility. Unless you're using a SAN or NAS, raw devices are always associated to the physical computer that hosts the device. This means that it is hard to move virtual machines that are installed on a physical device to another host computer.

Mounting virtual disk files

Because of the flexibility of the Linux operating system, some tools are available on Linux hosts only. The vmware-mount command is one of these tools. Using vmware-mount allows you to mount individual partitions from a VMware disk, irrespective of whether the disk resides in a .vmdk file or on a raw device. Because the Linux operating system has support for many filesystems (including Windows filesystems), you'll be able to mount virtually anything using vmware-mount.

Never use vmware-mount to access the disk of a virtual machine that is currently in use. If you do so, you risk making the virtual machine disk file inaccessible. So be sure to shut down the virtual machine before applying the following procedure.

The following procedure describes the approach for mounting partitions in a VMware disk file:

1. To start with, you need to find out which partitions exist within a disk. To find this out, use vmware-mount -p your-vmdkfile.vmdk. The following code listing shows what the result could look like. As you can see, you'll use vmware-mount on the master VMDK file as follows:

```
vmwarehost:/home/user/vmware/OpenSUSE 64-bit # ls *vmdk
OpenSUSE 64-bit-s001.vmdk   ...s005.vmdk   OpenSUSE 64-bit-
  s009.vmdk
OpenSUSE 64-bit-s002.vmdk   ...s006.vmdk   OpenSUSE 64-bit-
  s010.vmdk
OpenSUSE 64-bit-s003.vmdk   ...s007.vmdk   OpenSUSE 64-bit-
  s011.vmdk
OpenSUSE 64-bit-s004.vmdk   ...s008.vmdk   OpenSUSE 64-bit.vmdk
vmwarehost:/home/user/vmware/OpenSUSE 64-bit # vmware-mount
  -p OpenSUSE\ 64-bit.vmdk
Nr      Start        Size Type Id Sytem
-- ---------- ---------- ---- -- ----------------------
 1      2048    2263040 BIOS 82 Linux swap
 2    2265088   39677952 BIOS 83 Linux
vmwarehost:/home/user/vmware/OpenSUSE 64-bit #
```

2. In the previous code listing, you can see that two partitions exist within the virtual disk. Note the partition number because you'll need it to mount the partition. As in the previous code listing, only partition number 2 contains a Linux filesystem; this is the partition that should be mounted. Mounting the partition means that you have to make it accessible in the filesystem of the Linux host. In Linux this means that you'll have to connect it to a directory. To do this, you need to specify a couple of arguments to `vmware-mount`: the path to the disk file, the partition number, and the mount point in the Linux host's filesystem. For instance, this could be a command, such as `vmware-mount OpenSUSE\ 64-bit.vmdk 2 /mnt`.

3. After mounting the partition on the Linux host, you can access its files from the mount point and apply any changes that you would like to make to the file.

4. Once you have finished with the mounted disk file, you should unmount it as well. The easiest way to do this is using the `-k` option with `vmware-mount`, followed by the disk ID, as in `vmware-mount -k /OpenSUSE\ 64-bit.vmdk`. Note that this will only work if there are no open files in the mounted directory. If you get a warning stating "target is busy", you can also use `vmware-mount -K` on the VMDK disk file. This will force the disk file to unmount.

You can also mount virtual disks from the graphical menu. Select the virtual machine and navigate to **Settings | Harddisk | Utilities | Mounting** for a graphical interface that will allow you to mount the disks.

Managing VMware virtual disks

Another offline disk manipulation utility that VMware Workstation has to offer is `vmware-vdiskmanager`. You can use this option to perform different tasks, including resizing the disk, defragmenting the disk, or checking it for errors.

Apart from using `vmware-diskmanager`, you can also use an option from the graphical VMware Workstation menu by selecting the virtual machine and navigating to **Settings | Harddisk | Utilities**. You will find the defragment, expand, and compact utilities to perform the tasks discussed here from a graphical environment.

When using `vmware-vdiskmanager`, it's a good idea to tell VMware what kind of disk it is using the `-t n` option. The following disk types can be managed:

- `0`: A single growable disk
- `1`: A growable disk that consists of several 2 GB disk files
- `2`: A preallocated disk file
- `3`: A preallocated disk file that is split into several 2 GB files

- 4: A preallocated ESX-type disk file
- 5: A compressed disk file
- 6: A thin provisioned virtual disk as is used in ESX 3.x and later

If you don't know which disk type you need, you probably need type 0, which is the default type that is used by VMware Workstation.

A nice command to start with is vmware-vdiskmanager -e; it checks the disk for inconsistencies. You should use this command before performing any action on a virtual disk file; the following command would check a regular VMware Workstation disk file:

```
vmware-vdiskmanager -e -t 0 mydisk.vmdk
```

If the virtual disk is a local disk, you occasionally have to defragment it as well. To do this, use the -d option as in the following command:

```
vmware-vdiskmanager -d -t 0 mydisk.vmdk
```

Another useful command is the one used to expand a virtual disk so you'll have more usable disk space within the virtual operating system. Note that expanding a disk on the host level won't expand the filesystem in the virtual machine, so you will also need to apply instructions specific to the virtual machine's filesystem to expand the disk at that level. To expand a virtual disk, you need to use the -x file, as in the following command where the size of a preallocated disk file has been expanded to 40 gigabytes:

```
vmware-vdiskmanager -x 40G -t 2 mydisk.vmdk
```

Some other options are available with vmware-vdiskmanager; the type vmware-vdiskmanager helps you with a complete list of all options.

Summary

In this chapter, you've read about the way VMware Workstation is organized on the host operating system. You've learned about which services are used and which configuration files are created, and you've also read about some useful management tasks with regard to virtual disks. In the next chapter, you'll learn how to set up virtual networking on VMware Workstation.

5

Networking VMware Workstation

If you just want to do an easy installation of a virtual machine, you don't have to worry about VMware Workstation networking; every virtual machine you'll create will be able to reach other computers on the network. If you want to set up a test environment, networking does become important. In some cases you'll need the virtual machines to be on an isolated network, where in other cases you'll need to use multiple network interfaces in a virtual machine. In this chapter, you'll learn about the different scenarios for setting up VMware Workstation networks.

Using different networking modes

If you're setting up a VMware Workstation environment as a test environment, you need to configure the appropriate networking. In some cases, you want virtual machines to be connected directly to the physical network, just like if it was a normal machine. In other cases, you might not have the IP addresses available that are needed to connect each virtual machine directly to the physical network. And yet in other situations, you may have to set up a completely isolated VMware network. In the following sections, you'll learn how to accomplish these different scenarios in VMware Workstation. To match these different networking scenarios, VMware Workstation offers the following networking options:

- Bridged
- NAT
- Host-only
- Custom

You can find these options on the network settings of a selected virtual machine, as well as in the **Network Preferences** menu. There is also an option, **Lan Segment**, that allows you to define specific segments in your Local Area Network (LAN). For advanced features, such as bandwidth management, you can use the **Advanced** option in the **Network Settings**.

An important point to recognize when setting up virtual networks is that each virtual network needs to be represented by a network interface at the host level. This host level network interface allows a virtual machine to communicate to external networks, other virtual machines, and if so required, the IP stack on the host itself. The following diagram shows a schematic overview of this configuration:

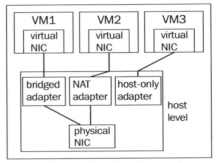

Virtual network schematic overview

Using bridged networking

If you want your virtual machine to be connected directly to the network, you need bridged networking. In bridged networking every virtual machine has its own IP address, and this should be an IP address that corresponds to the IP numbering plan in the physical network. This is because in bridged mode, you need to be able to address each node directly, from every other node in the network, no matter if this is a physical host or a virtual host.

In bridged networking, the VMware network adapter that is created at the host level doesn't do any filtering at all. It just works in bridged mode, which means that it arranges traffic to be sent over one physical interface by multiple virtual interfaces simultaneously. When setting up a virtual machine in a bridged mode, you need to make sure that the virtual machine's IP address matches the IP address that is in use in the physical network.

A special approach to the bridged networking option is replicate physical network connection. You can find this option on the network settings of a selected virtual machine. When using this option, the virtual machine replicates the exact state of the network adapter.

Using NATted networking

The default networking mode, is NAT (Network Address Translation). In NAT mode, the virtual machines are using IP addresses from a different IP subnet to the one in use on the physical network. The VMware network adapter works as a NAT network adapter. This means that it translates all packages that go out from the virtual hosts and replaces their IP address by the IP address of the NAT network adapter. Also, the NAT network adapter keeps track of all outstanding connections so that if an answer comes in for one of the virtual hosts, the NAT network adapter can translate the IP address back to the IP address of the virtual host.

Using NAT networking is the easiest way to set up networking in VMware and therefore, this mode is used as the default mode. It does, however, have the drawback that virtual machines cannot be reached directly from the outside. At the same time, this drawback is a benefit, because it protects virtual machines from security risks. However, because of the NAT translation, virtual machines can reach the outside network and they can receive replies to the packages they send out.

Using host-only networking

If you want to set up a test network for demo purposes, the host-only network is a useful choice. This network type creates an isolated network that won't be routed to external networks on its own dedicated IP address. While creating a host-only network, you can have the host participating in the network, which is useful if you want the network to be completely isolated and, therefore, be portable to the maximal extent.

Another advantage of the host-only network is that it works at all times, even if the physical network adapter is not connected. Especially on Linux, you risk the entire bridged or NATted network to go down if the physical network adapter is disconnected. This will never happen if you're on a host-only network.

Configuring virtual networks

To configure networking in VMware Workstation, you'll use the **Virtual Network Editor**. You can find this tool in the **Edit** menu of VMware Workstation (see the following screenshot). By default, it shows the three networks that are created at all times: a bridged network with the name vmnet0, a host-only network on vmnet1, and a NAT network on vmnet8. For each of the network types you can set some specific properties.

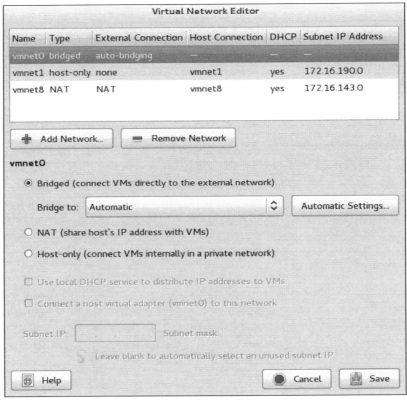

Specifying Virtual Network Properties

Setting bridged network properties

When using bridged network, you'll need to specify what network interface you want to bridge the virtual machines to. This is in particular important if you're on a laptop that has a LAN network interface as well as a Wi-Fi interface. The default setting is **Automatic**, which means that VMware Workstation tries to bridge VMs to the network interface that it detects as available. This doesn't always work well and therefore, you can specify that a virtual machine is always bridged to the same network interface, or that some interfaces are excluded from automatic bridging.

If you want to select a specific network interface to bridge the virtual machine to, you select this interface from the drop-down list that reads **Automatic** by default. Alternatively, click on **Automatic Settings** to deselect interfaces that you don't want to be used for automatic bridging.

For bridged networks, there is no need to specify the properties of a DHCP (Dynamic Host Configuration Protocol) server that hands out IP addresses automatically. Virtual machines on a bridged network will be able to communicate with the DHCP server on the physical network.

Setting host-only network properties

When using host-only networking, you can set up a DHCP service. This service is configured to hand out a range of IP addresses to virtual machines that are configured to automatically request an IP address from a DHCP server. By default, a DHCP server is configured for the host-only network, and an IP address range is assigned automatically. You can change these settings if required.

For some host-only networks, you might want to use fixed IP addresses only. If that is the case, you can switch off the local DHCP server for that network. You should pay attention to the IP address that you set for the host-only subnet. By default, VMware Workstation assigns an IP address for you, but that might not meet your internal networking requirements, so make sure to change this IP address to match your internal network requirements.

Another option related to host-only networking is to connect a host virtual adapter to this network. By default, the host network adapter is a part of the host-only network. In some cases, there is no need to include the host, and if that is the case for your environment, switch off the host network adapter here.

Setting NAT network properties

The properties that are assigned to a NAT network interface are similar to the host-only network configuration. What it comes down to is that you need to decide whether or not to run a DHCP service on the interface, and you can also select the subnet IP to be used. If you're not sure, it is fine to let VMware decide for you, it will make sure that an unused IP subnet is assigned so that you can connect virtual machines to external networks without any additional configuration.

To use networking in VMware Workstation, you'll get different new interfaces on your host. Every interface is assigned to the corresponding network in VMware. On a Linux host, you can use the command `ip addr show` to get a list of all the interfaces and the associated configuration.

```
vmwarehost:~ # ip addr show
1: lo: <LOOPBACK,UP,LOWER_UP> mtu 16436 qdisc noqueue state UNKNOWN
    link/loopback 00:00:00:00:00:00 brd 00:00:00:00:00:00
    inet 127.0.0.1/8 scope host lo
    inet6 ::1/128 scope host
       valid_lft forever preferred_lft forever
2: eth0: <BROADCAST,MULTICAST,UP,LOWER_UP> mtu 1500 qdisc mq state UP
qlen 1000
    link/ether b8:ac:6f:c9:37:8f brd ff:ff:ff:ff:ff:ff
    inet 192.168.1.125/24 brd 192.168.1.255 scope global eth0
    inet6 fe80::baac:6fff:fec9:378f/64 scope link
       valid_lft forever preferred_lft forever
3: wlan0: <NO-CARRIER,BROADCAST,MULTICAST,UP> mtu 1500 qdisc mq state
DOWN qlen 1000
    link/ether a0:88:b4:20:e9:f4 brd ff:ff:ff:ff:ff:ff
4: vmnet1: <BROADCAST,MULTICAST,UP,LOWER_UP> mtu 1500 qdisc pfifo_fast
state UNKNOWN qlen 1000
    link/ether 00:50:56:c0:00:01 brd ff:ff:ff:ff:ff:ff
    inet 172.16.190.1/24 brd 172.16.190.255 scope global vmnet1
    inet6 fe80::250:56ff:fec0:1/64 scope link
       valid_lft forever preferred_lft forever
5: vmnet8: <BROADCAST,MULTICAST,UP,LOWER_UP> mtu 1500 qdisc pfifo_fast
state UNKNOWN qlen 1000
    link/ether 00:50:56:c0:00:08 brd ff:ff:ff:ff:ff:ff
    inet 172.16.143.1/24 brd 172.16.143.255 scope global vmnet8
    inet6 fe80::250:56ff:fec0:8/64 scope link
       valid_lft forever preferred_lft forever
```

Use this command to troubleshoot network configuration problems.

Interfaces down

When on a Linux host the physical network interface is down, you'll risk all VMware network interfaces being down as well. If you need to set up a test network in VMware Workstation in which just the connection between the different virtual machines is required and no external connections, use host-only networking. This type of networking will always work, irrespective of the actual state of the external network interfaces.

Creating your own virtual network

By default, VMware Workstation gives you three virtual networks, one for host-only, one for bridged, and one for NAT networking. In some cases, you'll need to add other networks as well. This is the case if, for instance, you want to configure one of the virtual machines with two network cards, so that you can create a network bonding configuration in which two network cards create an environment for redundant networking. If you have requirements like this, you'll need to set up an additional network.

To add an additional NAT or host-only network, there are no specific requirements. If you want to add an additional bridged network, you must have a network interface that isn't used by a VMware bridged network adapter yet: you can only have one bridged network adapter per network card.

The following procedure shows how to do that:

1. From VMware Workstation, open the **Edit** menu and select the Virtual Network Editor. Click on **Add Network** to add a new network.

2. Select **Network name**. **vmnet0**, **vmnet1**, and **vmnet8** are in use by default, so select a number that isn't used yet. Also specify if you want to create a bridged, NAT, or host-only network. If you're creating this network to set up one of the virtual machines with a dual network interface, make sure that you select a network type that matches.

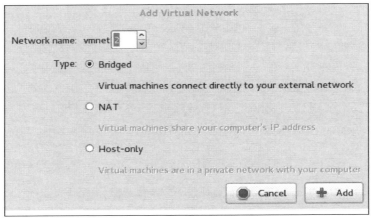

Creating a new VMware network

3. After adding the new interface, click on **Save** to write the configuration to the disk. The new interface is now ready for use.

Using advanced network properties on virtual machines

On virtual machines, you can specify how the network connection is to be used. In this section, you'll learn how to work with advanced properties of the network adapter, and you'll also read how to add multiple network cards to one virtual machine.

Setting advanced network properties on virtual machines

To specify advanced settings for the network cards in virtual machines, you first select the virtual machine properties. Next, select **Network Adapter** that is in use for your virtual machine. This will show all the current configuration parameters. From this interface, you can see the type of network connection that is currently configured, and if needed, you can change the default type here.

You'll notice that apart from the three default types, two additional types are available as well: **Custom** and **LAN segment**. You can use the custom network type to configure the virtual machine to use a network connection that you've created yourself. To select this network connection, make sure that the corresponding **vmnet** number is selected. Another option offered is **LAN segment**. This is a remainder of virtual machine teams, a feature that was offered from VMware Workstation 5.5 until 7.x that no longer exists. Don't configure this option, in VMware Workstation 9 it is of no use anymore.

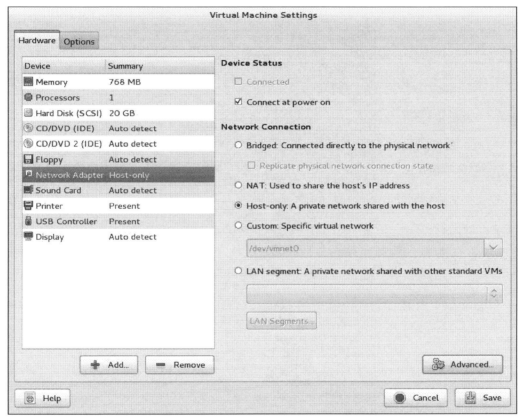

Selecting the virtual machine network connection

For each network adapter in a virtual machine, you can set some advanced properties as well. These are related to bandwidth that is offered on a virtual machine network interface, and acceptable packet loss rates. You can access these properties by clicking on the **Advanced** button.

Network adapter advanced properties

To communicate efficiently with other computers and devices in the network, it makes sense to specify the available bandwidth on a network card. By default, the **Bandwidth** is set to **unlimited** and there is nothing wrong with that if you're on a fast Gigabit network. If, however, you're on a network that is not that fast, it makes sense to set the **Bandwidth** to the speed of your connection. This helps establishing a connection with machines that are significantly slower or faster. To specify the bandwidth in use, you can either select the appropriate **Bandwidth** from the drop-down list, or manually specify the **Bandwidth** in kilobits per second (kbps).

Another property that you might want to set is **Packet Loss**. Some operating systems while installed as a virtual machine in VMware Workstation will show you packet loss on the virtual network card in the operating system. If you're using a Linux virtual machine, look at the error and dropped statistics, as shown by the ifconfig command:

```
linuxguest:~ # ifconfig eth0

eth0      Link encap:Ethernet   HWaddr B8:AC:6F:C9:37:8F
          inet addr:192.168.1.125  Bcast:192.168.1.255
Mask:255.255.255.0
```

```
inet6 addr: fe80::baac:6fff:fec9:378f/64 Scope:Link
UP BROADCAST RUNNING MULTICAST  MTU:1500  Metric:1
RX packets:23626 errors:8 dropped:56 overruns:0 frame:0
TX packets:5815 errors:4 dropped:381 overruns:0 carrier:0
collisions:0 txqueuelen:1000
RX bytes:13922479 (13.2 Mb)  TX bytes:482931 (471.6 Kb)
Interrupt:18
```

If you see a significant amount of erroneous or dropped packets, it makes sense to set **Packet Loss** on the virtual machine network card to approximately the percentage of lost packets. If VMware Workstation knows that a relatively large amount of dropped packets is to be expected, it helps if it can let the guest operating system know about that. If VMware Tools are installed in the guest operating system, the errors will be handled in a better way.

The last property that you can set on a network adapter in a virtual machine is **MAC Address**. By default, a random generated MAC address is used as the unique identifier for each network card. If you need the MAC address to be fixed to a specific address, you can do that here.

Using multiple network cards within a virtual machine

If in your virtual configuration, you want to test installing a server, you might want to configure it with multiple network cards to experiment with advanced server features, such as DMZ configurations or network bonding. Before you'll be able to configure the network cards from within the guest machine operating system, you'll need to present the network cards to the virtual machine. This is not too hard to do, but before you begin, it makes sense to clarify exactly what it is that you need:

- If you need to test with advanced security settings, for instance, to configure a virtual machine as a host in a DMZ, the virtual machine should have one network interface that is connected to the outside world, preferably by using a bridged network card. The other network card should be presented to a host-only network that is shared with other virtual machines that represent the internal network.

- If you want to test bonding configurations, where different network cards are joined together, you need to make sure that both network interfaces that you want to join in the bond are in the same type of network. If you want to bond interfaces in a bridged configuration, you need one physical device for each virtual network card.

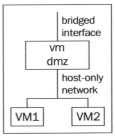

Virtual DMZ overview

Of the configurations previously discussed, the bonding configuration is definitely the more difficult one. This is because bonding is never something isolated; if you want to set up bonding in a virtual machine, at least one other node in the virtual network needs to be set up for bonding as well. You can also set up bonding between a virtual machine and the host operating system. To do this, follow the instructions of the host operating system for setting up the bond device from there. VMware Workstation does not offer advanced options for virtual switch configuration, so you cannot define the bond itself from VMware Workstation.

If you're using VMware Workstation to create a test environment that you want to import in vSphere, you should be aware of the limitations of VMware Workstation. As just discussed, VMware Workstation does not offer any virtual switch configuration options, so you need to test these features once the virtual machine is imported in vSphere.

Summary

Networking is an important part of setting up a test environment in VMware Workstation. In this chapter, you have read how to set up a virtual network test environment, using bridged, host-only, and NATted virtual network interfaces. You've also read how to set advanced features of virtual network cards on the virtual machines that you've created. In the next chapter, you'll learn how to access VMware Workstation, and the virtual machines it is running remotely.

6
Accessing Virtual Machines Remotely

When setting up a serious test environment, it may be useful to make the machines accessible from a distance. Even if you're using VMware Workstation on your own computer, there are different ways in which you can accomplish this. In this chapter, you'll read how to use VNC, the VMware web service, and VNC on individual machines to access virtual machines remotely.

If you're running a big test environment with multiple virtual machines, it can be useful to enable remote access. Generically speaking, there are three different methods to do this:

- The first method is by using the VMware web service. This approach allows you to enable access to all virtual machines that you're hosting in an easy way.

- The second method is by enabling VNC remote access on individual virtual machines.

- The third method is by using an external solution such as TeamViewer, which allows remote access to the host computer and everything running on it. This is great if the host computer doesn't run anything but VMware.

Setting up shared machines with the VMware Web Service

The VMware Web Service is an easy and convenient way to share machines with other users. To use this solution, you need to set up shared machines, but it's also a good idea to create a dedicated user account to share the virtual machines so that you can prevent remote users from getting access to the files on your computer. Be aware however that normal user accounts without administrator privileges won't be able to get access to other users' virtual machines. An administrator user can at least browse through virtual machines that other users have created. It is a lot easier to set up a dedicated account for the use of VMware Workstation, and from that account, share all virtual machines. This prevents you from the need to give too much access privileges to other users.

Shared virtual machines and user accounts

To use VMware shared virtual machines, you'll need a user account on the computer where the shared virtual machine resides. This means that before setting up the shared virtual machine, you'll have to create these user accounts — unless you want the remote user to connect with your own username and password.

Creating a Windows user account

If you're working in a corporate environment with Active Directory, all user accounts are probably already available. If you're running VMware Workstation on a Windows 8 computer, you'll need to set up a user account yourself. To do this, start the PC Settings application and click on **Users**. From here, select **Add a user** and follow the wizard to proceed through all of the required steps to create the user. You don't have to grant administrator privileges to the user, just create the user account and assign a password.

Creating a Linux user account

To create a Linux user account, open a shell window and make sure that you have root permissions. To escalate your permissions to the root level, use the `sudo so` command and enter the root password. Next, type `useradd -m username`. This adds the new user account to your computer. To set a password for this user, still as root, enter the `passwd` command and enter the new password twice.

Sharing a virtual machine

Probably the easiest way to enable shared VMs is by using the VMware integrated feature. This allows you to run a web service on the host's operating system, which gives access to all virtual machines on that host. Enabling the VMware Workstation Server starts at the virtual machines that you want to provide access to. You'll first have to share the virtual machine, after which the workstation's server properties can be set. The procedure described as follows shows how this works:

1. Right-click on the virtual machine that you want to share. Select the **Manage** menu, and click on **Share**.

2. To enable sharing for the selected virtual machine, you need to make it available in the shared VM's directory. You can do this by either moving the virtual machine, or making a full clone of it. If you choose the latter option, you will basically make a full copy of the virtual machine, which means that the cloned virtual machine is going to be an independent machine. This choice is useful if you want to be able to do different things in the share machines than what you're doing in the original machine. If you move the virtual machine, it's just the physical location that is moved. You won't experience it from the VMware Workstation interface; it's just a protection issue. The benefit of moving the virtual machine rather than cloning it is that you will work on the same virtual machine.

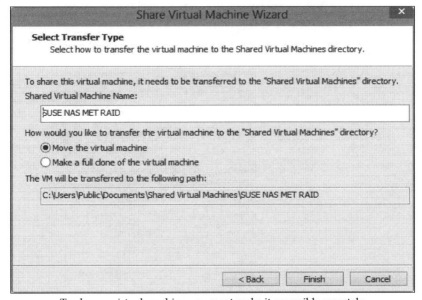

To share a virtual machine you must make it accessible remotely

3. After sharing it, you'll see a new folder with the name **Shared VMs** in VMware Workstation. You'll also notice that the virtual machine is still accessible from the `My Computer` folder as well.

Accessing a shared virtual machine

Accessing a shared virtual machine from a remote computer that runs VMware isn't difficult. The following procedure describes how you can do it:

1. To access a shared virtual machine from another computer that's running VMware Workstation 9, you'll use the **Connect to Server** option from the **File** menu. Enter the name or IP address of the computer that shares the virtual machine, and enter a name and password to access the shared virtual machine.

2. It is likely that at this point you'll get a security certificate warning. This warning is generated because probably the remote virtual machine isn't registered in a corporate network, and that is fine; just ignore the warning and click on **Connect Anyway**. To prevent this warning from popping up again, select the **Always trust this host with this certificate** option as well.

3. After successful authentication to the remote computer, it will be added to your VMware Workstation view, including all the shared virtual machines that are running on it. If you are planning to use the shared virtual machines on a frequent basis, it's a good idea to click on **Remember** in the dialog that asks if you want to remember the login information for the remote computer, so that you'll see the virtual machines the next time after starting VMware Workstation (provided that the remote machine is available).

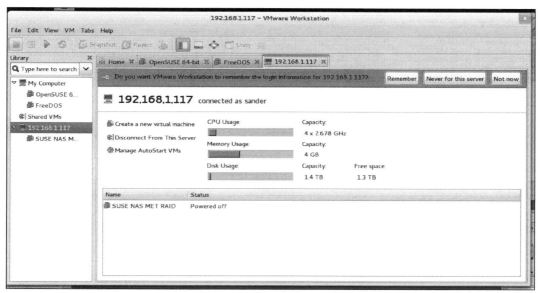

Accessing remote shared virtual machines

Using VNC for remote virtual machine access

In the previous section, you have learned how to create shared virtual machines within VMware. This option is useful if you want to share virtual machines with other users who are also using VMware. On the other hand, to access shared virtual machines from a remote computer that doesn't run VMware, this approach doesn't work and you will need something else. **VNC** might be a good solution.

VNC is a generic protocol that you can use on any operating system to provide remote access. It works from physical computers as well as virtual machines. To open a virtual machine for VNC access, you can use the setup procedure for your specific operating system. Alternatively, you can also use the VMware Workstation virtual machine options to enable VNC access. In this section, you'll learn how to configure the VMware Workstation using VNC.

Before starting to configure VNC on your virtual machines, you should consider the alternatives. VNC is great if you want to connect to a remote graphical desktop but if you want to access a virtual machine that runs in the console-only mode, you don't need it. In that case, use SSH or any other console-based virtual machine access method. It's easier to set up and is also more secure.

Enabling VNC access on a virtual machine

To enable VNC access on a virtual machine, you should open the virtual machine's properties. To do this, select the virtual machine and navigate to **VM | Settings**. Next, open the **Option** tab. On this tab, click on **VNC Connections**. The current status should be set to **Disabled**. Click on **Enable** to open VNC access for the virtual machine and select the port you want to use. Every virtual machine needs a dedicated port assignment. For the first VM that you'll share with VNC, the default port 5900 will do fine. All subsequent virtual machines need a dedicated port however, so choose port 5901 for the second virtual machine, 5902 for the third, and so on. To add some extra protection, you can add a password as well. Next, click on **OK** to save the settings.

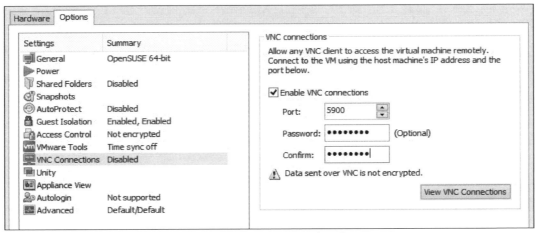

Enabling VNC access to virtual machines

Connecting remotely to virtual machines using VNC

To establish a remote connection to a virtual machine that is shared with VNC, you need a VNC Viewer. You can download a free VNC Viewer at www.tightvnc.com/download.php. After downloading it, run the setup procedure. There is no need to do anything difficult, just select the default settings. The installation program gives you a VNC Viewer as well as a VNC Service. You can use the VNC service to provide remote access to your computer's desktop. You don't need it to connect to individual virtual machines on remote computers, but make sure to provide a password to the service to prevent unauthorized use.

After installation, you need the TightVNC Viewer to get access to VNC-enabled virtual machines. In the remote host box, enter the IP address of the computer that hosts the VNC shared virtual machine. Next, enter the port assignment as well. For the first virtual machine you want to connect to, you can use the default port assignment 5900; if you want to connect to any other virtual machine, you need to specify the port to the IP address, as in 192.168.1.117:5901, and click on **Connect**. If you have protected VNC access with a password, enter the password now and click on **OK**. You'll now be connected to the virtual machine.

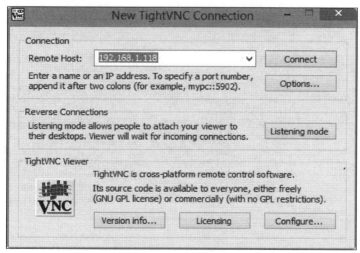

Connecting to a VNC enabled virtual machine

Once you've established a remote connection with the VNC enabled virtual machine, there may be specific buttons or key sequences that you need. At the top of the VNC Viewer window, you'll see a button bar. In this bar, you'll find access to commonly used function keys for use within the virtual machine. These include all keys that have a special function both in the virtual machine and in the host operating system, such as *Ctrl*, *Alt*, and *Ctrl + Alt + Del*. Use the buttons if you need to use these keys within the virtual machine.

Once you've finished working in the VNC session, you can just close the VNC Viewer window. As the remote machine is running somewhere else, the only thing you have to do is just disconnect the session.

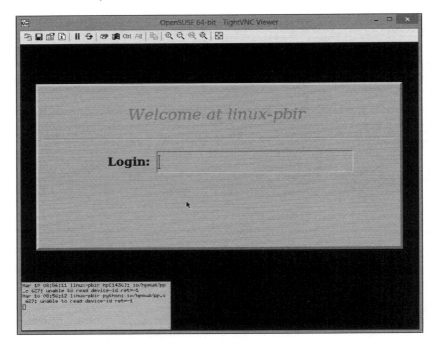

Using TeamViewer for remote access through a firewall

The solutions discussed so far are provided by VMware Workstation, and they work fine as long as you're not behind a NAT router. NAT routers typically protect machines on the internal network, which means that no one from outside can reach them. If you want to share virtual machines or their content with users on external networks, TeamViewer provides a nice solution.

TeamViewer (www.teamviewer.com) consists of an agent that you'll run on the machine to which you want to give access, as well as a client program. As long as it is for personal use, both components are available for free. In a VMware environment, you can run the TeamViewer agent both on the virtual machine and in the host operating system.

Installing the TeamViewer agent

The most flexible way to work with TeamViewer is by installing the TeamViewer agent on the host computer. This means that remote users get complete access to the entire host so that they can start VMware Workstation and run virtual machines from within VMware Workstation. If that scenario seems a bit too insecure for you, you can also install the TeamViewer agent in one or more virtual machines to provide access to those specific virtual machines. The following procedure describes how it works:

1. Go to www.teamviewer.com/en/download and download the TeamViewer host.
2. Run the installation wizard and follow all prompts. Once completed, the TeamViewer host program shows a user ID. Give this ID to anyone who needs remote access to your host or virtual machine.

Using the TeamViewer client

On the remote client that needs to access the virtual machines, you'll need to install the TeamViewer full version. You can download this version for free from www.teamviewer.com. Install the TeamViewer full version on your computer and accept the default values as proposed by the installation wizard.

Once installed, TeamViewer shows an option to access a remote computer. To use this option, you need to enter the remote session's ID that is provided by the TeamViewer host agent. Enter it and click on **Connect** to partner to establish the session. You'll now have complete access to the remote machine.

Accessing VMware Workstation from tablets and mobile devices

Unlike VMware ESXi, there is no application for either iPad, Android, or Windows to access VMware Workstation remote machines in an easy way remotely. This doesn't mean that you're without any options though; there are VNC clients for tablets, and there's also a TeamViewer client that allows you to access a VMware Workstation virtual machine or host remotely. So accessing a VMware Workstation virtual machine from a tablet is not much different from accessing a virtual machine from a regular computer. Just install the VNC client or TeamViewer client and follow the procedures described earlier in this chapter.

Summary

In this chapter, you have learned how to share virtual machines and enable remote access. You have learned that there are many ways to access virtual machines from a distance, including VNC Viewer, TeamViewer, and the VMware Workstation shared virtual machines feature.

In the next chapter you'll learn how to convert and import virtual machines.

7
Converting Virtual Machines

Among the major benefits of using virtualization is how easy it is to migrate machines. In VMware Workstation, you can use both physical to virtual (P2V) migration, as well as virtual to virtual, which allows you to import virtual machines that have been created somewhere else. In this chapter you will learn how to use both techniques.

Converting physical machines to VMware Workstation

To convert physical machines to a virtual machine, you need vCenter Converter Standalone. This product is available for free and you can easily install it from VMware Workstation 9 or any later versions. You should be aware of some limitations though, such as:

- VMware Converter Standalone runs on Windows only, so you cannot use it to convert virtual machines that are running on Linux computers

- VMware Converter Standalone in a VMware Workstation environment does not support remote conversions

- To convert a virtual machine, you should install VMware Converter Standalone on that virtual machine, and apply the procedure described in the following section

Virtualizing a physical Windows machine with VMware Converter

To convert a physical machine that runs with Windows using VMware Converter Standalone, you first have to download and install the VMware Converter Standalone utility. You can download it for free at www.vmware.com.

Before starting a P2V conversion of a Windows computer, you need to switch off **User Account Control**. The following procedure describes how to do this:

1. Open the Windows Control center and select **User Account | Change User Account Control Settings** (or select the **User Account Control** settings application on Windows 8).

2. Move the slider to **Never Notify** and click on **OK**.

3. Now you need to enable the **Run all administrators in administrator approval mode** option in the Windows security policy. To do this, open a **Run** window using Windows key + *R* and enter secpol.msc.

4. Select **Local Policies | Security Policies**.

5. Select **User Account Control: Run all administrators in administrator approval mode** and enable this option.

6. Restart your computer.

    After its installation, you can use the **Virtualize a Physical Machine** option to convert a physical machine into a virtual machine. The following procedure describes how to perform the P2V virtualization from the standalone utility that is installed on the physical computer that you want to convert. Notice that the **Virtualize a Physical Machine** option that you'll find in the VMware Workstation **File** menu doesn't work.

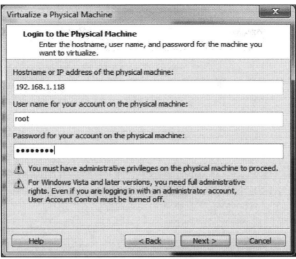

The Virtualize a Physical Machine option doesn't work

7. From your computer's desktop, select **VMware vCenter Converter Stand-alone client**.

8. As you can also use this tool to connect to a VMware Server that is running on another computer in a vCenter environment, you first have to select which server you want to use. Choose between either connecting to a local server or a remote server. Select the **Connect to a local server** option:

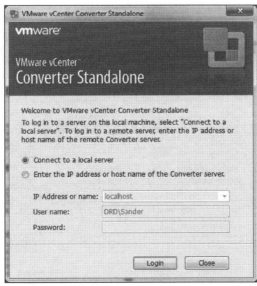

To convert virtual machines to VMware Workstation, select Connect to Local Server

9. In the window that opens now, click on the **Convert Machine** button. To perform a physical-to-virtual conversion, next select **Powered-on machine** and select **This local machine**—it is the only option that works in a VMware Workstation environment.

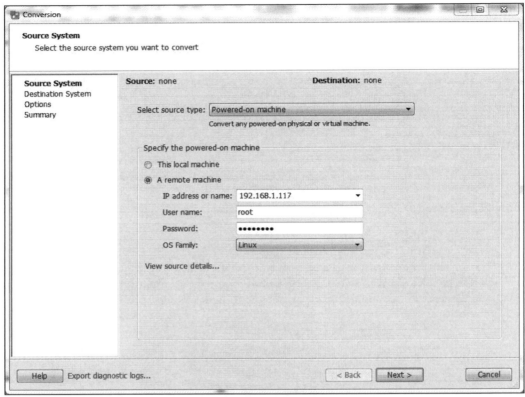

Connecting to the target machine

10. After selecting the local machine, you have to select the destination type. That is the type to which you want to convert this physical machine. Make sure that the destination type VMware Workstation or another VMware virtual machine is used, and next select **VMware Workstation 8.0.x** from the drop-down list. This works for VMware Workstation 8.0 and higher. Also, select a name for the virtual machine and the location where you want to store the virtual machine files. Notice that you will store the virtual machine's file on the local machine, that is, the machine where VMware vCenter Converter is running.

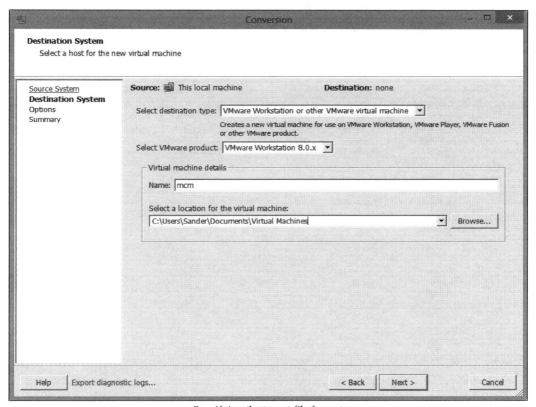

Specifying the target file format

11. In the next window, you'll see an option window where you can specify how the hardware on the physical machine should be represented within the virtual machine. You'll probably see some warnings as well, indicating options for which enough resources are not available. To make sure the P2V conversion works, tune all hardware options of the physical machine to settings that will work within the virtual machine as well. Ensure that you have at least a look at the following options:

   ○ **Memory: by default**: The virtual machine will have the same amount of memory as the physical machine. You may need to reduce this.

   ○ **Post-conversion**: You probably want to install the VMware tools automatically on the virtual machine once it has been converted.

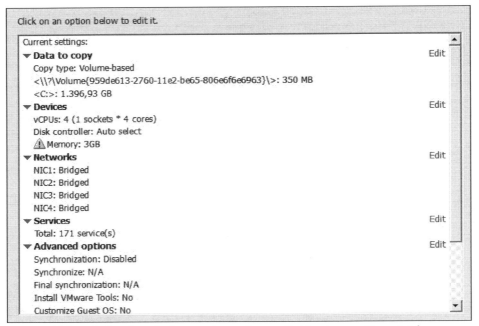

Before starting the actual conversion, make sure that hardware settings match

12. After changing all hardware settings, click on **Next**. This shows a summary of all the selected parameters. On this summary window, click on **Finish** to start the conversion. Notice that depending on the size of the physical machine, it may take a long time to complete this process. You'll see the conversion task being added to the vCenter Converter tool, with an indication of the approximate time it is going to take before the synchronization process is completed. You can monitor the conversion process from the VMware vCenter Converter Standalone console window. Make sure that it can complete without any errors.

Once the conversion process is completed successfully, the VMDK file of the virtual machine is copied to the disk on the computer that runs VMware Workstation. The next step is to import the virtual machine disk file into your VMware Workstation computer. Later in this chapter you can read how this works.

Performing a physical-to-virtual conversion of computers running Linux

Although the previous versions of VMware supported P2V on Linux virtual machines, this is no longer the case in the current versions. Therefore, you'll have to rely on other solutions to do P2V for Linux virtual machines. The easiest way is to use a pure Linux solution for updating virtual machines: you'll boot the Linux machine from a Linux boot disk, convert all of the physical disk to a virtual disk image, and next you'll import the disk image in VMware as described in the following sections.

 The following procedure describes how to do Linux P2V on a system that has one hard disk only. It is possible to do P2V on a system that has more than one hard disk, but this is much more difficult and not explained further. If you understand this procedure, you can use it to create several disk files and import these disk files in VMware.

To perform the following procedure, you'll need a Linux boot disk. It is recommended to use Knoppix; you can download a free ISO image of Knoppix from www.knoppix.org. This Linux boot disk is used to take an image of the physical disk. Next you'll need an external disk to store the image that you're going to write. Before you start, make sure that the external hard disk has lots of free disk space; you need to create a file on it that is as big as the entire hard disk of the physical machine.

1. Start the physical machine that you want to convert from the Knoppix DVD.

2. In Knoppix, you will be logged in automatically. Open a console window and enter the `sudo su` command, which gives you administrator (root) permissions in the Linux operating system.

3. Use the `cat /proc/partitions` command. This shows you which disks and partitions currently exist on the Linux operating system that is installed on the Linux computer. It should show you a device with the name `/dev/sda`, and some partitions that you can recognize as `/dev/sda1`, `/dev/sda2`, and maybe more (this depends on how the computer has been installed).

4. Connect the external USB disk to your computer and use the command `cat /proc/partitions` again. You'll notice that a disk has been added. This is the external hard disk. It is very likely that the name of the disk itself is `/dev/sdb`, and it has a partition with the name `/dev/sdb1`. (This is likely if the computer that has been converted only has one disk.)

5. Use the command `mount /dev/sdb1 /mnt`. This makes the external hard disk accessible on the `/mnt` directory.

6. Use the following command to start the cloning process: `dd if=/dev/sda of=/mnt/mydisk.img bs=1M`. You will need approximately 1 hour for every 50 gigabytes, and depending on the speed of your computer and external disk, this can be much more. So better not wait for it.

7. Once the procedure has been completed, use `umount /mnt` to unmount the external disk. You have now stored the disk image file and can import it in VMware.

Performing a V2V conversion and virtual machine import

In the preceding sections, you've learned how to convert a physical computer into a virtual machine. Occasionally, you'll also need to import virtual machine files in VMware Workstation. This can be because you have copied a VMDK file from another computer to your VMware Workstation computer, but you may also need this approach to import a virtual machine file that has been created on another virtualization platform. In this section you'll learn how to perform both of these tasks.

Importing raw image files into VMware Workstation

The easiest way to convert a raw disk file to VMDK is by using the vmware-vdiskmanager utility. You can use this tool both on the Linux as well as the Windows versions of VMware. The following procedure demonstrates how to convert a raw disk file to VMDK:

1. Attach the medium that contains the raw disk file that you have created to your computer, and make sure it is accessible by either a drive letter (Windows) or a filesystem mount (Linux).

2. Use the following command to start the conversion:

   `vmware-vdiskmanager -r inputfile.img -t 1 outputfile.vmdk`

3. Wait until the conversion has finished before proceeding to the next section.

Importing VMDK files into VMware Workstation

Once you have converted the source disk file to the VMDK format, you can create a new virtual machine based on the VMDK file. This procedure is more or less the same as the procedure of creating a new virtual machine. What it comes down to is that you start creating a new virtual machine and tell the installation wizard to use an existing VMDK file. The following steps demonstrate how it works:

1. Start VMware Workstation and navigate to **File | New virtual machine**.

2. Select **Custom** when asked what kind of configuration you want to use.

When asked for the type of configuration you want to use, select Custom

3. Select **I will install the operating system later** when the **New Virtual Machine Wizard** window opens.

4. Specify the guest operating system that is on the VMDK file, and customize all hardware you want to use, up to the point where the installer asks what kind of disk you want to use.

5. When asked what disk you want to use, select **Use an existing virtual disk**:

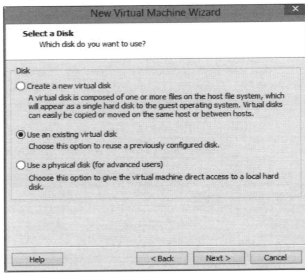

To import a VMDK in VMware Workstation, you need to use an existing virtual disk

6. You'll now see an interface where you can browse to an existing disk file. Click on the **Browse** button and navigate to the location where the disk file is stored. If the virtual machine consists of multiple VMDK files, make sure to select the first VMDK from the list.

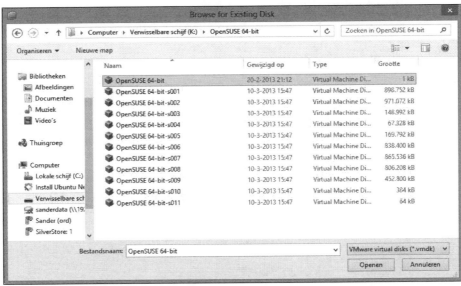

If the VMDK consists of multiple files, select the first of these files

7. You can now finish the VM creation procedure by clicking on **Finish**. This creates the virtual disk file for you.

Importing other disk file formats into VMware Workstation using OVF

There are many disk file formats that can be used by different virtualization products. Among these are the following:

- **OVF**: This stands for **Open Virtualization Format**; this is a generic virtual machine disk file that is supported by many virtualization solutions
- **VDI**: This is the Virtual Box native disk format
- **VMDK**: This is the VMware native disk format
- **VHD**: This is the Virtual Hard Disk format that is mainly used in Microsoft environments
- **HDD**: This is the Parallel Hard Disk format
- **QED**: This is the QEMU-enhanced disk
- **QCOW**: This is the QEMU Copy-on-Write format

Within VMware Workstation, there is not much support for all of these different disk file types. Some other virtualization solutions, though, offer reasonable-to-good support to export virtual machines into a file format that VMware can read. In the procedure described as follows, you can learn how to export a virtual machine from Virtual Box so that it can be imported in VMware Workstation.

1. In Virtual Box, make sure that the VM you want to export is shut down.
2. From the **File** menu, select **Export Appliance**.
3. Select the virtual machine you want to export and click on **Next**.
4. Make sure that the virtual machine is exported to a file with the `.ova` extension. This is an archive file that can contain multiple OVF files. Click on **Next** after specifying the filename to be exported.
5. Click on **Export** to start exporting the virtual machine.

Once you have exported the virtual machine to the appropriate target format, you need to import it into VMware Workstation. To do this, from VMware Workstation, click on the **File** menu and select **Open**. Now, browse to the location where you've saved the OVA file and open it. The Import Virtual Machine dialog opens now. In this dialog, you can enter a name and destination storage path for the virtual machine. Provide the name and path and click on **Import**:

Importing an OVF file

At the first attempt to import the virtual machine, it will fail. This is because the virtual machine file, by default, does not meet the virtual hardware compliance checks. If you now click on **Retry**, the import process will start again and you will succeed to import the virtual machine.

Once the virtual machine has been imported, make sure that the Virtual Box tools are uninstalled from the virtual machine and install the VMware tools. The VM you just imported is now ready to use.

Importing third-party virtual machines using VMware vCenter Converter

Apart from the methods discussed in preceding sections, VMware vCenter Converter can also help to import some virtual machine types from external programs. Different file types are supported, such as Microsoft Virtual PC, Microsoft Hyper-V virtual machines, and parallel virtualization products. You can select the specific machine types in the **Select source type** drop-down list in the first screen of the VMware Converter conversion window. After specifying the source of the virtual machine file, you'll just browse to the virtual machine file. The **Browse** window gives access to all the supported virtual machine files; if your virtual machine file isn't listed by default, it's not supported.

Before starting the V2V conversion project in VMware vCenter Converter, you can also check the contents of the virtual machine file. Click on **View Source Details** to see a **Machine Details** window for the selected virtual machine:

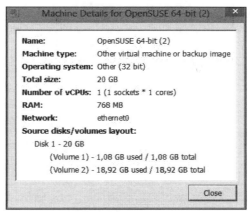

Verifying virtual machine contents

After verifying the virtual machine's contents, you'll proceed through the conversion wizard to select VMware Workstation as the destination type, and provide a name and location for the virtual machine file. Before the start of the actual conversion process, you'll see the virtual machine's properties. Click on **Edit** to tune the virtual machine's contents to your needs and start the conversion process.

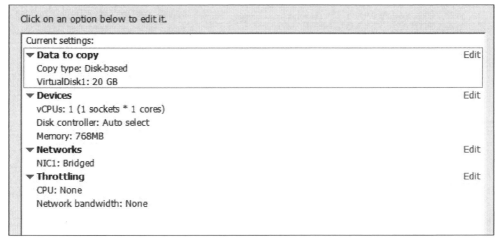

Before starting the conversion, you can change properties of the virtual machine

Summary

There are many ways to convert virtual machines, but there is no "one-size-fits-all" solution. Before performing either a physical-to-virtual or virtual-to-virtual conversion, you'll really need to check if the type of conversion you need is supported. If it is not, you can check the logfiles to find out why there have been problems. Fortunately, inside and outside VMware, almost all conversions are supported. In this chapter, you've read how to perform P2V and V2V from Windows and Linux to VMware.

8

Cloning and Snapshots

In a test environment, it is often necessary to deploy virtual machines rapidly and to revert to a previous state in an easy way. VMware Workstation provides all the tools that are required for this purpose. In this chapter, you'll learn to work with cloning and snapshot tools that enable you to perform these tasks.

Understanding when to apply which tools

A **snapshot** is a photo of a state of a virtual machine. As a virtual machine often requires a lot of work before a desired state of the machine is reached, it is a good idea to take a picture of that exact state. If something goes wrong at a later stage, having a snapshot makes it possible to easily revert to the previous state of the virtual machine. So the base concept of working with snapshots is to make it easier to revert to a previous state.

A **clone** is a copy of a virtual machine. Using clones is convenient if several virtual machines are needed, with more or less the same configuration on each virtual machine. By cloning a virtual machine, you'll make a copy of the actual state of a machine. After making the clone, you'll just have to modify the properties of the virtual machine that need to be unique on that machine.

In some ways, clones and snapshots are closely related. This is because you can create a clone of a snapshot of a virtual machine, but you can also clone the current state of a virtual machine, which in fact creates a snapshot of the virtual machine. To understand this, you need to understand the difference between a linked clone and a full clone.

In a **linked clone**, only modifications are stored. This means that if something happens to the original state of the virtual machine (for example, the VM files get corrupted), the linked clone gets corrupted as well. It is, however, an approach that is very efficient with regard to available disk space. As only modifications are stored in a linked clone, the disk space requirement is minimal. Creating a linked clone is also a very fast process.

A **full clone** is like a complete copy of a virtual machine. Creating a full clone is a much longer process as the entire virtual machine disk has to be copied over. It requires more disk space as well, but the benefit is that a full clone creates an independent virtual machine. Therefore, you're better off with full clones if you need a maximum amount of flexibility. In the following sections, you'll learn how to work with snapshots and clones.

Working with snapshots

In this section, you'll learn how to create snapshots of virtual machines. You'll also learn how to use the Snapshot Manager to manage a setup where different snapshots are used.

Creating snapshots

To create a snapshot, you don't have to do anything with the virtual machine. You can create a snapshot irrespective of the actual state of the virtual machine, so it doesn't matter if it is currently active or not. If the machine is powered on, the current state of the virtual machine memory is included in the snapshot as well. This is a useful feature as it allows you to return to the exact state the machine was in while taking the snapshot.

To create a snapshot of a virtual machine, select the virtual machine first. Then from the VM menu, navigate to **Snapshot | Take snapshot**. Here you are presented with a small dialog box where you can enter a short description of the snapshot. You should always enter some description as it may be clear now what the snapshot is being used for, but you probably won't know it anymore if you have a look at the virtual machine a few months later. Also, having a clear description for a snapshot makes it easier to identify the right snapshot in the Snapshot Manager.

To make identifying the snapshot easier at a later stage, enter a clear description of what it is being used for

Once the snapshot process has started, it will take a while to complete. You will see a progress bar in the lower-left part of the virtual machine window if it has been activated. In theory, you can just continue working in the virtual machine; in practice, you'll notice that it is slow and sometimes even very unresponsive. It's better to wait a while and give the snapshot process a few minutes to complete.

The actual files of the snapshots will be created in the directory where the VMDK files of the virtual machine are stored. For each VMDK file, you'll find a snapshot file as well. You'll notice that the snapshot file is smaller as it only contains the modifications that were made since the last snapshot was taken; or if this is the first snapshot you have taken, it will contain the differences from the original virtual machine.

RHEL61-000003	25-3-2013 20:06	VMware virtual dis...	1 kB
RHEL61-000003-s001	25-3-2013 20:34	VMware virtual dis...	18.240 kB
RHEL61-000003-s002	25-3-2013 20:34	VMware virtual dis...	3.840 kB
RHEL61-000003-s003	25-3-2013 20:34	VMware virtual dis...	343.808 kB
RHEL61-000003-s004	25-3-2013 20:34	VMware virtual dis...	28.224 kB
RHEL61-000003-s005	25-3-2013 20:34	VMware virtual dis...	80.512 kB
RHEL61-000003-s006	25-3-2013 20:34	VMware virtual dis...	4.864 kB
RHEL61-000003-s007	25-3-2013 20:34	VMware virtual dis...	14.016 kB
RHEL61-000003-s008	25-3-2013 20:34	VMware virtual dis...	15.552 kB
RHEL61-000003-s009	25-3-2013 20:34	VMware virtual dis...	896 kB
RHEL61-000003-s010	25-3-2013 20:34	VMware virtual dis...	320 kB
RHEL61-000003-s011	25-3-2013 20:34	VMware virtual dis...	64 kB

For each VMDK file, a corresponding snapshot file is created

Reverting a snapshot

The goal of creating a snapshot is that at any moment you can easily revert to the previous state of a virtual machine. The easiest way to do this is using the **Revert to snapshot state** option that you can find at **VM | Snapshot**. This option allows you to easily get back to the last snapshot that you have created on a virtual machine. Reverting to a previous snapshot resets the virtual machine to its previous state, and you'll know for sure that all changes that have been made since have been lost. Also, while reverting to the state prior to the snapshot, you will be unable to use the virtual machine and hence lose connection. A much more sophisticated method to revert to a previous state is using the Snapshot Manager.

Using autoprotect snapshots

A special kind of snapshot is the **autoprotect snapshot**. This is a snapshot that is created automatically every day. If you want to use autoprotect snapshots, you'll have to enable them for each virtual machine that you want to use them on. This doesn't happen automatically because you need disk space to store the autoprotect snapshots. Using autoprotect costs a minimum of 3 GB for every virtual machine.

To enable autoprotect, apply the following procedure:

1. Select the virtual machine that you want to use autoprotect for.
2. From the VM menu, open the **Settings** item and click on the **Options** tab.
3. On the **Options** tab, select **Enable AutoProtect** and specify how you want to use it.

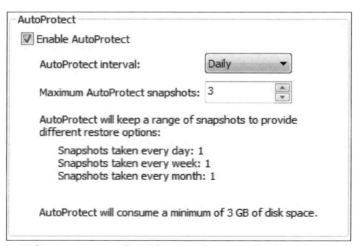

With autoprotect, you'll enable a sort of automatic backup schedule

When using autoprotect snapshots, it is important to realize that autoprotect doesn't just create one snapshot everyday and keep that around for a couple of days. By default, autoprotect creates a snapshot everyday, and it keeps three different autoprotect snapshots: one that allows you to go back one day, another one that allows you to go back one week, and a third that allows you to go back one month. It is possible to have autoprotect create more than just three backups, but you'll need to make sure that you have the required amount of disk space to store all these snapshots.

Snapshots and powering off

Using autoprotect snapshots helps you create an automated backup solution for your virtual machine. Another way of creating snapshots automatically is using the option to create a snapshot when a virtual machine is powered down. On the **Options** tab of the **Virtual Machine Settings** window, you can find the **Snapshot** option. This option allows you to use the following options:

- **Just power off**: This option will do nothing and just power off the virtual machine.

- **Take a new snapshot**: Use this option if you automatically want to take a snapshot of a virtual machine every time you power it off.

- **Revert to snapshot**: Use this option if you never want to keep the modifications that have been applied to a virtual machine. Using this option is very useful in educational environments where you want a virtual machine to be started in a clean state at the start of each class.

- **Ask me**: This option asks the user if a snapshot must be taken or if a reversion to the last state of the virtual machine has to be done.

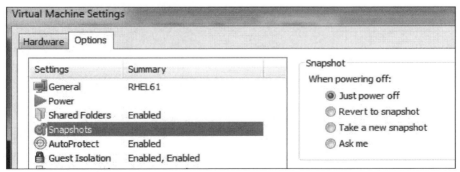

When powering off the virtual machine, you can automatically either revert to a previous snapshot or take a new snapshot

Working with the Snapshot Manager

The Snapshot Manager allows you to work with snapshots in the most flexible way. You can use it to revert to any virtual machine state, start from there, and build a completely different configuration so that you can create two development branches based on a specific snapshot state and decide which solution fits you best.

You can find the Snapshot Manager by opening the virtual machine you want to manage and navigating to **VM | Snapshot | Snapshot Manager**. You'll now see the Snapshot Manager with all the snapshots that have been created for this virtual machine.

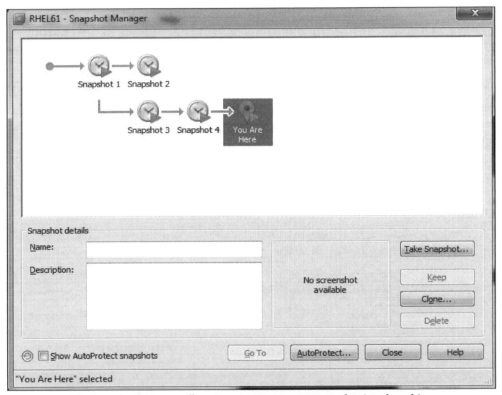

The Snapshot Manager allows you to revert to any state of a virtual machine

Working with snapshots from the Snapshot Manager is not hard to do at all. You'll just select the snapshot that you want to start from and restore it (irrespective of whether there are snapshots that have already been created based on the selected snapshot). Once restored, you can continue working on the virtual machine from the selected snapshot state.

By default, in the Snapshot Manager you don't see autoprotect snapshots. Even if the Snapshot Manager shows an option that displays autoprotect snapshots as well, it is probably not a good idea to do that. You'll typically use the snapshots in Snapshot Manager to walk back a clearly defined path in the snapshots on your system. In autoprotect, there isn't really a plan, and even more importantly, the snapshots are removed automatically. Therefore, you should make sure to never create a snapshot that is based on an autoprotect snapshot.

Creating clones

A snapshot is a virtual machine that is in a specific state. When working with snapshots, there will still be one virtual machine that can easily be restored to a specific state. The major difference between a clone and a snapshot is that a clone is a new virtual machine that is independent of the original virtual machine. Even if there is some relation between a snapshot and a clone (for instance, you can create a clone based on a snapshot), a clone basically is a new virtual machine. This means that once you have created a clone of a virtual machine, you can even start creating new snapshots of that virtual machine.

When creating clones, you really need to think well about what you want to use them for. If you just want to use them for your own convenience, a linked clone is the best solution. It can be created very fast, and it takes the least possible amount of disk space while it still offers full functionality. The major difference though is that you'll never be able to copy it as an independent virtual machine to another computer. If you need to do that, you'll need a full clone.

There are different ways to create clones. No matter which method you use, you will have to make sure that the virtual machine is shut down before you can make the clone. This requirement exists because the virtual machine files cannot be modified while the cloning is in process. The most important reason for this is that VMware Workstation is used on a Linux host or Windows platform where filesystems are used that do not allow virtual machine files to be modified by different processes at the same time. You'll need a VMFS filesystem in a VMware ESXi environment if you want to be able to clone a virtual machine without shutting it down first.

The most direct way of creating a clone is by using the **Manage** option in the VM menu. From this menu, select the **Clone** option to start the Clone wizard. The first step of the clone wizard asks where you want to create the clone from. This can either be from the actual state of the virtual machine or from a snapshot, if it has been created. If no fit snapshot exists, the wizard will show an error, indicating that it's not possible to create a clone based on a snapshot for the selected virtual machine.

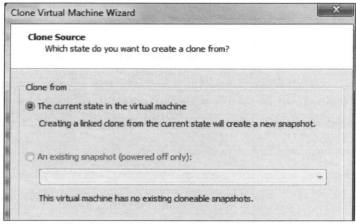

Selecting on the basis of what you want to clone

After selecting what you want to create the clone on, you'll need to select between either a linked clone or a full clone. You have to realize that a full clone is a complete copy of a virtual machine, so you'll need the same amount of disk space that is used by the virtual machine as available disk space on the host computer. So if the virtual machine uses 60 gigabytes of disk space, you'll need at least 60 gigabytes of disk space on the host as well!

After verifying that you have the required amount of free disk space, you can start the cloning process. In the last step of the wizard, specify the name that you want to assign to the clone as well as the location on the host operating system where the clone has to be stored. Once created, the clone will show in the VMware console as a new virtual machine, and that is also how it is to be considered.

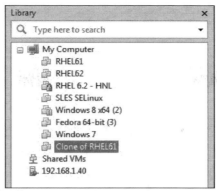

A cloned virtual machine appears as a completely new virtual machine in the VMware Workstation library

Another way of creating clones is using the Snapshot Manager. The advantage is that using Snapshot Manager, you can easily select a snapshot that you want to create a clone of. Just select the snapshot state you want to use and click on the **Clone** button.

Preparing virtual machines before cloning

If you're creating clones of Linux virtual machines, the procedure is rather easy. You just have to start the cloning process; once the process has been completed, there are a few items that need to be changed. You can just change these one by one. Typically, on a Linux virtual machine you need to be sure to change the following to create a new identity for the cloned virtual machine:

- The hostname
- The IP address
- The entry for this host in /etc/hosts

After changing these, you will need to restart the virtual machine to make sure it picks up on the new identity.

On Windows, changing the identity of a virtual machine is more complicated. The main reason for this is that the Windows license is bound to the identity of a Windows virtual machine. To make sure that you'll be compliant with the Windows license that you've purchased, you should generate a new identity and enter a new license code for it. The most versatile way to do this is to use **Sysprep**; it resets Windows to the state it was in when it was started for the first time. In the following section, you can read how to use Sysprep on Windows to create a template of your Windows virtual machine.

Using Sysprep on Windows to create a template

On Windows, the procedure is much more complicated as the identity of a Windows machine is not just in a few configuration files; it is all over the Windows virtual machine. That is why Microsoft has created Sysprep, a tool that allows you to create a base image of a virtual machine. You'll typically find this tool in any Windows installation under the location, `c:\Windows\System32\sysprep`.

You generally don't want to run Sysprep on a virtual machine that already has lots of things installed. The aim of Sysprep is to create a template of a new virtual machine; this makes it easier to deploy new virtual machines based on the Sysprep template.

After installing the Windows virtual machine that has a basic configuration, start the Sysprep tool and make sure you select the **Enter System Out of Box Experience** option. This puts your Windows installation in a mode where all personalized information is removed, and Windows behaves as if it has been started for the first time. Also make sure to select **Shutdown** as the shutdown mode (you want the virtual machine to be shut down after the completion of the Sysprep procedure) and select the **Generalize** option.

Make sure to select **Shutdown** as the default shutdown mode. By default, **Restart** is selected. Using this mode, you can restart the virtual machine, and once it restarts, the reconfiguration will be started automatically. This is not what you need, because the purpose of sysprepping a virtual machine is to remove all the specific configuration from it.

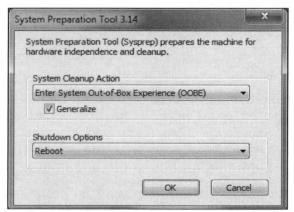

Before cloning Windows, you should run the Sysprep tool

Once the virtual machine has been sysprepped, open the **Settings** window for the virtual machine from the VM menu, click on the **Options** tab, and on that tab, click on **Advanced**. From here, navigate to **Settings | Enable Template** and click on **OK**.

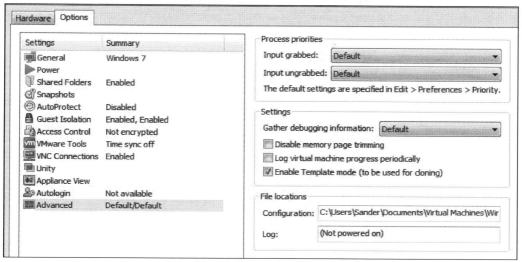

On a sysprepped virtual machine, you should enable the template mode

After setting the template mode, you'll first have to create a snapshot of the virtual machine. Once you've done that, you can clone the virtual machine. In the clone wizard, make sure to select the option to create a clone based on a snapshot — you'll notice that this is the only available option anyway because the virtual machine is in the template mode.

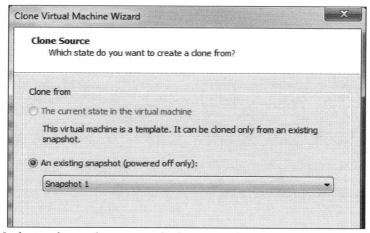

In the template mode, you can only clone a snapshot and not the current state

In the remainder of the process, you can choose whichever option you want to use—they are not really important for the cloning process to complete. When you start the virtual machine again, it will start in the same way a Windows instance starts on a new computer. This means that you'll need to enter the license information first and then provide all the other details required to configure the virtual machine.

Backups in a virtual environment

In this chapter, you've learned how to use snapshots and clones. Because of these features, you don't really need backups in a traditional way (in which a backup program is scheduled to copy files from a filesystem to an offline medium) anymore. If you enable a feature such as autoprotect snapshots, a backup is created automatically every day. There are a few things to consider however, before thinking that you're completely secure when using features such as clones and backups. The most important considerations are listed as follows:

- No matter how good your cloning and snapshot strategy is, as long as they are on the same disk as the original virtual machine files, you can hardly consider these virtual machines fully protected. In a good backup scheme, files need to be copied to another medium, and if possible, even to another site.

- A clone is just a copy of a virtual machine. The longer back that the clone was created, the less you can consider it a decent backup of a virtual machine. Clones are useful to make working with virtual machines easier, but you should not consider them backups.

- An autoprotect snapshot is what comes closest to a real backup. It at least protects you from errors within the virtual machine. But still, you need access to the original virtual machine files.

Summary

In this chapter, you learned how to work with snapshots and clones in a versatile test environment. Using these techniques makes it possible to easily deploy new virtual machines and save the current state of virtual machines. You have also read about how to change the identity of virtual machines after cloning, and how to handle the cloning process in the case of Windows where the actual state of the virtual machine is closely related to the license that you have acquired for Windows.

In the next and last chapter of this book, you'll learn how to use VMware Workstation as a tool to enable the sharing of virtual machines with others in a cloud environment.

9

Sharing Virtual Machines

In a test environment, a virtual machine is a convenient way to share your test results with others. VMware Workstation offers many options to share. You can upload virtual machines to vSphere or make them available in the cloud by using the VMware Marketplace. Also you can share virtual machines with other users that use VMware Player. To make it totally clear to the users what they can do with their virtual machines, you can also make screen movies from the test results you've accomplished in your virtual machines to explain to others what you have been doing. In this chapter you'll learn how to use these techniques.

Uploading virtual machines to vSphere and the cloud

VMware Workstation is used by many to create and test virtual machines in an isolated environment before uploading them to the production environment. This is made easier by the option to upload virtual machines directly to vSphere and ESXi. To use this functionality, it doesn't matter if you're in a vSphere environment with unmanaged hosts, or if you have hosts managed by vCenter Server, both environments are supported.

Making virtual machines ready for vSphere

Even if VMware Workstation and vSphere come from the same vendor, there are some significant differences between the two solutions. The most important difference relates to networking, so it makes sense to develop a plan with regard to the networking architecture before starting to upload virtual machines to vSphere.

There are big differences between the networking options that are offered by vSphere and the networking in VMware Workstation. The differences might seem so significant that it appears impossible to mirror the state of networking that you want to use in vSphere in a VMware Workstation environment. Depending on the kind of networking that you're looking at however, there are some options nevertheless.

The most significant networking feature that is available in vSphere and not in VMware Workstation, is the **virtual switch**. VMware Workstation doesn't allow you to connect a virtual switch, on which advanced network settings can be specified. Also, there is no distinction between the management network and the production network that you normally see in a vSphere environment. There are good reasons why these features are missing however.

An ESXi Server in a vSphere environment typically has a minimum of at least eight network cards, in some cases even more. VMware workstation is developed to be used on desktop computers and a typical desktop computer just has one network card available, or two if it's a laptop with an Ethernet network card as well as a WiFi network card. Even with this limitation, VMware Workstation still has much to offer. Even if the physical host may have one network card only, you can easily create virtual machines that have several network cards. This allows you to set up an environment where the virtual computer routes traffic from the physical network to which the host is connected to an internal host-only network, which allows you to emulate a setup where a DMZ is used.

This topology mirroring is exactly what you can do in a very useful way in VMware Workstation. So if you're looking for a solution that allows you to play with advanced vSwitch features, including VLAN tagging, VMware Workstation is not ideal to use as a pre-production test environment. If you're looking for a solution that is easy to understand and allows you to build a test networking topology, VMware workstation is the perfect solution.

To mirror network topologies, VMware Workstation offers three different kinds of network adapters, all of which can be created with the Virtual Network Editor. By default three networks have already been created and as an administrator, you can add up to a total of 10 virtual networks. That means that even if the host has only one network adapter, you can have as many as 10 different network adapters in any virtual machine!

Two of the network types that are available in the Virtual Network Editor allow for a direct connection to the external network. These are the **NAT** and **bridged network type**. The most open method is to provide virtual machines with a bridged network adapter. Using this, the virtual machine is connected directly to the external network. This means, for example, it will get an IP address from the DHCP server on the physical network and it also means that you'll need to make sure that resources are available on the external network. If, for instance, you use a network bridge on the network interface that connects your host to the Internet, the Internet provider has to be willing to hand out an additional IP address. This limitation means that a bridged network interface is not useable in all scenarios.

As an alternative, you can use the NAT type network interface. Use this type if you don't manage the external network, and no configuration is available to connect the virtual machines directly to the external network. Using NAT has a disadvantage though, as while using NAT you cannot access services on the virtual machines from the external network. NAT, however, is also commonly used in corporate vSphere implementations to add an extra level of protection to services on the internal network, which shouldn't be accessible from the outside, and as such, NAT might be a welcome addition to your network configuration anyway.

The third network type is **host only**. This means that on the host, the virtual network card is in no way connected to a physical network card, so the host-only network card cannot be accessed from any machine outside the host-only network. This may sound like a limitation, but host-only networks offer some real benefits. You could, for example, configure one virtual machine with a public network interface, which is connected to the external network by using NAT or bridged mode, and at the other side of that virtual routing hosts, create one or more host-only networks, which reflect the internal company network, and even a DMZ network. To make that work, you need to configure routing processes on that virtual machine though, to have it do the work that would normally be done by a (virtualized) router in your infrastructure.

Uploading virtual machines to vSphere

Once you have ensured that the features you need in vSphere can be prepared in VMware Workstation, you can start uploading the virtual machines. VMware Workstation supports both, the uploading of a virtual machine to an individual ESXi host as well as connectivity to a vSphere environment that is managed from the vCenter Server. To upload to an ESXi host, enter the name or IP address of the host you want to connect to and to upload to the vCenter Server, enter the IP address or name of the vCenter Server that manages the vSphere environment.

To start the upload from the VMware Workstation menu, navigate to **File | Connect to Server** and enter the IP address, administrator name, and password that you need to connect to the vSphere Server. You'll now see an overview of the current vSphere environment, displaying current usage, resource availability and which virtual machines are actually being used.

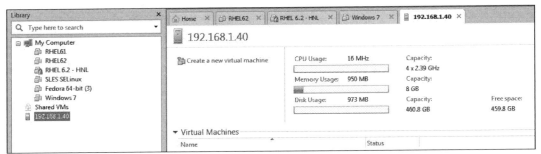

An overview of the current usage of ESXi Server

To copy a virtual machine over to the vSphere environment, from the VM menu, select the **Manage** option and from there choose **Upload**. This presents you with a new window in which you can select the vSphere environment you have just connected to. After clicking on **Next**, from the drop-down list you can select the specific ESXi Server in your vSphere environment that you want to copy the virtual machine to. Also make sure to specify which data store you want to use before clicking on **Finish** to copy over the virtual machine.

Selecting where to copy the virtual machine to

Once the virtual machine has been copied, you're ready to start using it in the vSphere environment.

Sharing virtual machines with VMware Player

VMware Player is a free VMware product that allows others to create virtual machines and import virtual machines that have been created by others. It is typically the product that you want to provide to other users who need to be able to use virtual machines that you have created. VMware Player users can create virtual machines as well, but the solution lacks the advanced features that are typically appreciated by power users, such as the option to create snapshots. VMware Player is available as a free and independent product on www.vmware.com, but it is also installed as a part of VMware Workstation.

Preparing to move virtual machines to VMware Player

Before sharing your virtual machines with VMware Player users, it is a good idea to test if the virtual machines work as you want them to in the VMware Player environment. Just start VMware Player from the computer where VMware Workstation is installed, and click on **Open a Virtual Machine**. Next, browse to the location where the VMX file of your virtual machine is stored and click on **Open**. The virtual machine is now added to the VMware Player interface.

Opening existing virtual machines in VMware Player

From VMware Player, you can easily use the virtual machine and all of its features. You will notice though that the advanced VMware Workstation features are missing. Amongst the significant missing features is the option to create snapshots or work with snapshots. That means that you'll need to decide which state of the virtual machine you want to use before sharing it with a VMware Player user; that user won't have the ability to easily switch to another state of the virtual machine.

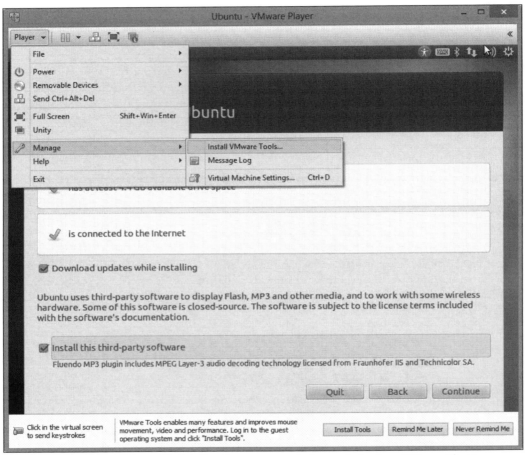

Compared to VMware Workstation, there are many features missing from VMware Player

Making a virtual machine available to a user of VMware Player is easy. Select the directory where the virtual machine files (VMX as well as VMDK) are stored and copy it over to the computer of the VMware Player user. Once the files are stored on that computer, the VMware Player user can just import the virtual machine.

Starting a copied virtual machine for the first time

After copying a virtual machine and starting it for the first time, you might get a few questions. To start with, depending on the state that the virtual machine was in when it was first copied, VMware Player may tell you that the virtual machine appears to be in use. It is easy to fix this issue; just click on **Take Ownership**. This allows your local VMware Player to take ownership of the virtual machine and do anything you like with it. At this point you can start the virtual machine.

After starting the virtual machine for the first time in VMware Player, you will be asked if the virtual machine has been copied over or moved. This is to avoid a situation where a duplicate MAC address is used in an environment. If you select **I moved it**, you keep the MAC address that was in use in the virtual machine. When you select **I copied it**, a new MAC address will be generated to avoid conflicts with other virtual machines that are using the same MAC address. In the latter case, you might have a problem accessing the network from the newly copied virtual machine.

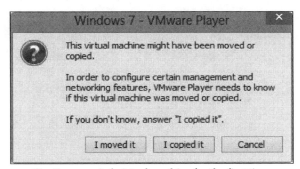

Starting a copied virtual machine for the first time

If you cannot access the network from a virtual machine that you've just copied over, the best solution is to shut down the virtual machine and remove the current network card and add a new one. This will force the operating system to create a new network card and all the configuration that is needed on it, which allows you to connect to the network from a copied virtual machine.

Using VMware appliances

Instead of creating all the virtual machines yourself, you can also use virtual appliances. A virtual appliance is a ready-to-use virtual machine that you can download from the VMware Marketplace at `solutionexchange.vmware.com`.

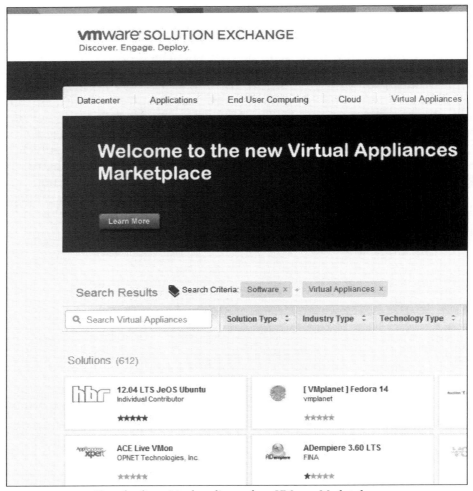

Downloading virtual appliances from VMware Marketplace

On every virtual appliance that you find on the VMware Marketplace, there is a **try now** button. Click on it to get access to a download page where you can access the compressed virtual machine files. After downloading these files, you can copy them to the `Virtual Machines` folder and open them in VMware Workstation of VMware Player like you would do with any other virtual machine that you've just copied over.

If you really want your virtual machines to be available for a broad public, you can apply for a virtual appliance partnership. After getting this partnership (which will not be free), you can build an appliance according to the VMware specifications and upload it to the Marketplace. From there, anyone can download it and install it in their VMware environment.

Making screen movies

If you really want it to be clear what to do with your virtual machine when sharing it with others, you may like the **Capture Movie** feature that you can find in the VM menu for every virtual machine. This feature allows you to capture movies of everything you do on a virtual machine. Especially if used with a voice-over that explains what you are doing, the **Capture Movie** feature is extremely useful.

Before starting to capture a movie, it is a good idea to enable sound. This allows you to use the microphone on your computer to add explanation about what you're doing. By default, no sound is enabled in VMware Workstation movies.

To add sound, you need to change the contents of the config.ini file. If you're using a Windows host, you can find this file in C:\ProgramData\VMware\ VMware Workstation. In this file, add the line mks.movie.config.high. recordSound="TRUE" and restart VMware Workstation.

The config.ini file is in the hidden directory ProgramData in C:. Make sure to enable Windows Explorer to show hidden files before trying to access the file. To save changes to this file, you need administrator permissions. Select and right-click on Notepad, and select **Run as Administrator**. You can now open the file and add the above line to it.

Before starting to capture a movie in VMware, you need to be aware of an important limitation: it works in graphical mode only. That means that if you want to capture a movie on a Linux environment that is showing a text-only desktop, you'll just see the initial screen of the desktop and none of the modifications. This is a well-known issue that up to now hasn't been fixed. So if you want to capture screen movies in VMware workstation, start your Linux machine in graphical mode.

Before starting to capture, put the virtual machine in the exact state where you want to start capturing. Then navigate to **VM | Capture Movie** and select the name and location of the file you want to create. After doing that, perform all the manipulations that you want to be recorded.

Once finished, go to the VM menu again and click on **Stop Capture movie**. The screen movie is stopped at this point and will be saved to the disk.

While capturing a movie, a record button is shown in the lower-right part of the virtual machine window

Before sharing the screen movies that you've created, it is a good idea to optimize the video a bit. No one likes looking at a badly created movie, where the presenter isn't really sure of what he's doing and makes lots of mistakes. So make an investment in good video editing software, cut all of the less successful bits of the movie, and maybe even enhance it with some picture in picture effects to make it a more appealing movie to look at. After doing that you'll be ready to share it with other users who will be able to understand what you wanted to accomplish with your virtual machine.

Summary

In this chapter you've learned what you can do with your virtual machines after creating them. You can upload them to different locations, such as vSphere, VMware Player users, and even the VMware Marketplace where other users can download your appliance. You have also learned how to create screen movies that explain to users of your virtual machine how they should use the features that you've embedded in them.

Index

Thank you for buying
VMware Workstation – No Experience Necessary

About Packt Publishing

Packt, pronounced 'packed', published its first book "Mastering phpMyAdmin for Effective MySQL Management" in April 2004 and subsequently continued to specialize in publishing highly focused books on specific technologies and solutions.

Our books and publications share the experiences of your fellow IT professionals in adapting and customizing today's systems, applications, and frameworks. Our solution based books give you the knowledge and power to customize the software and technologies you're using to get the job done. Packt books are more specific and less general than the IT books you have seen in the past. Our unique business model allows us to bring you more focused information, giving you more of what you need to know, and less of what you don't.

Packt is a modern, yet unique publishing company, which focuses on producing quality, cutting-edge books for communities of developers, administrators, and newbies alike. For more information, please visit our website: www.packtpub.com.

About Packt Enterprise

In 2010, Packt launched two new brands, Packt Enterprise and Packt Open Source, in order to continue its focus on specialization. This book is part of the Packt Enterprise brand, home to books published on enterprise software – software created by major vendors, including (but not limited to) IBM, Microsoft and Oracle, often for use in other corporations. Its titles will offer information relevant to a range of users of this software, including administrators, developers, architects, and end users.

Writing for Packt

We welcome all inquiries from people who are interested in authoring. Book proposals should be sent to author@packtpub.com. If your book idea is still at an early stage and you would like to discuss it first before writing a formal book proposal, contact us; one of our commissioning editors will get in touch with you.

We're not just looking for published authors; if you have strong technical skills but no writing experience, our experienced editors can help you develop a writing career, or simply get some additional reward for your expertise.

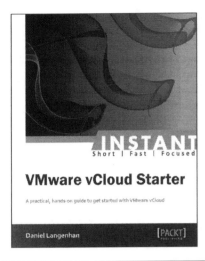

Instant VMware vCloud Starter

ISBN: 978-1-84968-996-0   Paperback: 76 pages

A practical, hands-on guide to get started with
VMware vCloud

1. Learn something new in an Instant! A short,
   fast, focused guide delivering immediate
   results

2. Deploy and operate a VMware vCloud in your
   own demo kit

3. Understand the basics about the cloud in
   general and why there is such a hype

4. Build and use templates to quickly deploy
   complete environments

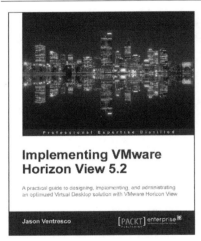

Implementing VMware Horizon
View 5.2

ISBN: 978-1-84968-796-6   Paperback: 390 pages

A practical guide to designing, implementing, and
administrating an optimized Virtual Desktop solution
with VMware Horizon View

1. Detailed description of the deployment and
   administration of the VMware Horizon View
   suite

2. Learn how to determine the resources your
   virtual desktops will require

3. Design your desktop solution to avoid potential
   problems, and ensure minimal loss of time in
   the later stages

Please check **www.PacktPub.com** for information on our titles

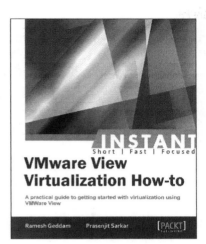

Instant VMware View Virtualization How-to

ISBN: 978-1-84968-916-8   Paperback: 76 pages

A practical guide to getting started with virtualization using VMWare View

1. Learn something new in an Instant! A short, fast, focused guide delivering immediate results

2. Implement virtualization on Windows 8

3. Learn details that are not available in the VDI documentation of VMware View

4. Learn about the advanced features of VMWare View 5.x

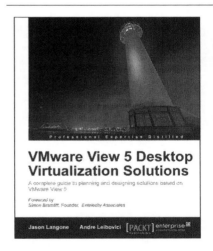

VMware View 5 Desktop Virtualization Solutions

ISBN: 978-1-84968-112-4   Paperback: 288 pages

A complete guide to planning and designing solutions based on VMware View 5

1. Written by VMware experts Jason Langone and Andre Leibovici, this book is a complete guide to planning and designing a solution based on VMware View 5

2. Secure your Visual Desktop Infrastructure (VDI) by having firewalls, antivirus, virtual enclaves, USB redirection and filtering and smart card authentication

3. Analyze the strategies and techniques used to migrate a user population from a physical desktop environment to a virtual desktop solution

Please check **www.PacktPub.com** for information on our titles

Made in the USA
San Bernardino, CA
19 August 2015